Colin Turner is an internationally acknowledged leader in the field of human potential. Combining Eastern philosophy and contemporary Western experience into a practical format for daily use, his thought-provoking lectures blend Universal Principles and Spiritual Growth with the commercial realities of life. His programmes and books which include the bestsellers, *Born to Succeed*, *The Eureka Principle*, *Financial Freedom* and *Swimming with Piranha Makes You Hungry*, have inspired people worldwide and his principled approach to business has been embraced by leading organisations.

*Also by Colin Turner*

**Born to Succeed**
**The Eureka Principle**
**Swimming with Piranha Makes you Hungry**
**Financial Freedom**

# Made For Life

## A compelling story of the human spirit's quest for fulfilment

Colin Turner

**CORONET BOOKS**

The right of Colin Turner to be identified as the Author of
the Work has been asserted by him in accordance with the
Copyright, Designs and Patents Act 1988.

First published in Great Britain in 1997 by InToto Books
Published in 1998 by Hodder and Stoughton
A division of Hodder Headline PLC

A Coronet paperback

10 9 8 7 6 5 4 3 2 1

A CIP catalogue record for this title is available
from the British Library.

ISBN 0 340 72887 6

Printed and bound in Great Britain by
Clays Ltd, St Ives plc

Hodder and Stoughton
A division of Hodder Headline PLC
338 Euston Road
London NW1 3BH

To my mother

# Made for Life

**A compelling story of the human spirit's
quest for fulfilment**

"Why *did* you kill yourself?"

It was the second time the voice had asked the question. The man did not want to answer, but words came anyway.

"What else could I have done?"

"You gave up," the voice returned impassively.

"It wasn't my fault, I had no choice!" He tried to defend himself. "I'd tried, really tried, but every time I started to find anything good in my life something came along to spoil it."

"Perhaps you could have *tried* harder, you had plenty of talent?" The voice made a statement out of a question.

"Yes, plenty of it, but I was never given the chance to use or develop it! If only I had been given more opportunity, just one, I could have made it."

"You already had the appropriate spirit, strengths, talent and ability to achieve your specific purpose in life. That's what you were made for. A human being; not a human doing.

By definition you must seek what you are to be and become it. Not just spend your life *doing* to get by; hoping and wishing that something will turn up which may suit you." The voice paused, the man became conscious of the silence, the darkness.

"Where an eagle will soar majestically above the earth, the tiny lizard scurries beneath a rock. Both are living out rôles which are perfectly natural for their purpose, meaning and contribution. The spirit of the eagle is appropriate and the spirit of the lizard is appropriate. So it is with you.

"If the eagle did the job of a lizard, would it feel frustrated? Of course! Because it would always feel that there was something not quite right... that it was capable of greater heights. Its natural sense of belonging would become an unnatural state of longing for something else."

"That's how I felt!", the man said. "I knew there was something I would be good at, but there wasn't anyone to show me the way."

"There was *always* someone, for there is no stronger soul to direct you than that of your own." The voice was louder, moving closer, then gently it began again.

"Let us talk further, for it is true that although each living person has their own combination code to the meaning and purpose they seek, they are blind to the understanding necessary to solve it.

"Although intended to be a school for souls our physical life on earth has followed a path which has blocked the flow of certain knowledge. This wisdom, which guides our spirit, needs to be rediscovered and understood. There are periods when, purposely, your spirit seeks a physical host which helps it to grow, to raise itself. Your story started even before you were born"

"Are you saying that I actually chose my life, chose to be me?" The man had forgotten how little he had wanted to talk. Now it became a need. His excitement contrasting with the calm undulating voice.

"Life has many levels and there are definite factors that determine its course. A certain dynamic of your spirit sought out the type of culture, environment and beliefs, before this birth, because it was these that it was ready to experience."

"You say a *certain* dynamic of my spirit made the choice, what does that mean? Why would I, or my spirit as you called it, choose what it did? It was *not* what *I* wanted. I would have preferred to be someone completely different to me and I'm sure I could have experienced more, as you say, if I had made a better choice."

"It is important to understand", the voice continued, placing stress on certain words and helping him to understand, "that the spirit has no attachment to the expression of *comp-*

*arison.* The spirit knows that it can be likened to a single wave in an ocean of waves. Some are larger, while others are smaller, but every one is part of one, unified state. Each drop of water can be taken and used independently yet still retain the characteristics of water. Regardless of the container it occupies, it is in its element.

"On the physical level, however, various indoctrination, which have developed culture and beliefs, develop an unnatural state of comparison. Your spirit would not recognise one body as better or worse than another. Its *focus* is to occupy a state which will allow it to develop further.

"This means expressing its potential on a physical plane, which in turn will allow greater absorption of experience. Like the water, the spirit is able to bring to its container all the dynamics essential to realise the potential that a physical host can achieve. Integrated within the very spirit of every man, woman and child is a dynamic to achieve its own specific purpose.

"The fundamental strengths, vital to the realisation of this dynamic, would be able to be developed effectively in the chosen physical host. Which is partly why it is chosen. It is another dynamic, however, which acts as an *ignition*, and a third that guides you to what you are to become. This dynamic, this essence of spirit, is like a *key*."

The voice paused. The man took advantage of the moment to consider the words and their meaning. He felt cheated, as if he had been left out of some huge secret that had been obvious to everyone else, but him. "But, why didn't I know what I was meant to achieve. Why wasn't I told in some way?"

"When we incarnate in a physical body", resumed the voice, "and are assaulted by the pains and pleasures which can only be felt on the physical plane, we forget our true nature and purpose. We view ourselves as just mind and body, with likes and dislikes, and not as spirit with meaning and purpose. If a key is unable to ignite, how can any process start? Quite simply, it cannot.

"It is, for this metaphorical reason, that your spirit chose an environment and culture which was perfect for the adversity it required to raise its level. Similar to the rainbow, which appears through adverse weather, the spirit's true colours begin to shine through adversity. Adversity is the spirit's catalyst for growth."

The man's thoughts flew to his childhood. Recollections did not come easily, as he searched for his earliest memory. He felt a sadness, as if something had been taken away from him and, for a moment, a pain as if something or someone was making him feel sorry for ever having what had just been taken away. It was hard to concentrate and the image he was trying to hold was unclear.

"But, if the spirit is already able to direct itself towards its purpose, why, then, does it look for problems to overcome in order to grow, in fact, why does it need to grow at all?" He had always found comfort in the habit of asking 'But' questions. They gave him time to think, or was it, he wondered, his way of trying to justify his thoughts?

"Again, similar to a rainbow," the voice seemed to understand the man's difficulty, "where seven colours spring from pure light, there are seven centres of consciousness to make up pure spirit. When pure spirit passes through the particular process, in order to feel physical expression, it occupies the level of evolution it has attained so far.

"Your spirit must seek to raise its level through obstacles in the same way that water can only raise its level by meeting an obstacle. Its natural tendency is to flow down but whenever it meets a barrier it has to raise its level to get over it—it cannot continue until it has overcome the barrier. Can you see that the bigger the barrier or obstacle, the higher its level is raised to get over it?

"The spirit's ultimate aim is to attain the highest level of consciousness, in order to regain the source from whence it came, in a stronger, more evolved form. To achieve its aim the spirit needs to transcend various levels of consciousness. It achieves this through physical experiences which will allow it to learn and teach love.

"Your parents had a make up, an environment, culture and beliefs that would influence the way in which they viewed and coped with you in your early years. The level of friction or harmony which existed would have been considered by the spirit as a perfect incubatory environment to provide the lessons it needed from which to learn.

"The degree to how much you chose to learn, embrace or resist lessons emanating from this environment is relative to how much you grow and the direction in which you move. In other words, your external world is relative to your internal world—as within; so without. Think about your 'world'?"

Once again, the man sought his memories. Nebulous recollections moved through his mind like old, blurry photographs. Slowly, there came clarity as a moving picture developed. He was experiencing a particular event, again, but this time as an observer, watching himself.

*"Do you have to be so hard on him and do you have to keep blaspheming? He will copy you!"* His mother often spoke to his father in this way, a sing-song combination of chiding and pacifying him. She wasn't a big woman, yet not small, just motherish, with a kind face that always held an anxious yet expectant expression.

*"He has to learn to do as he's told and what the hell is blasphemous about hell?"*, his father retorted. He was slapping paint onto the back door and his brush emphasised the 'hells' with an extra energy.

This was how the usual bickering began, with each one seeking to score points. It would end with barbed sentences which were not meant, but they couldn't stop themselves from saying. Even though each knew it would hurt the other.

His father could be a kind man but it seemed only when it suited him, or when others were pandering to his wishes. It was the frustration, which he wore on his face, that explained his short temper.

What struck the man, in seeing those tantrums now, was that his father had never seemed to follow the instructions he continually delivered. He would often moan out his favourite cliché about how life had 'dealt him an unjust set of cards', to which his mother would retort that it was not what you got, but how you played them, that mattered. This inevitably would start them off again.

It was almost like a ritual that they needed to perform, in order to confirm their security; their identities. Each seemed to want to control the other. There was a need, more than a want, in the relationship and it was a need based on habit.

It was weird watching himself, the man thought, and, yet, he felt quite relaxed by being able to observe in this detached way. It allowed him the opportunity to be objective, and the chance to perceive his parents differently.

His mother was a Christian and would have liked to have gone to church more regularly than they did, but apart from Events such as Harvest Festivals, Christmas, and Easter, any attendance was usually motivated by his father. Usually, when he felt the need to ask God for something because things were not going very well and when he was particularly worried.

It was at this time that the family atmosphere became even more tense. Shouting and complaining seemed to be their way of releasing tension. Both of his parents seemed to constantly find fault with one another, and their children. On the few occasions when praise was due, it was given grudgingly, with an embarrassment caused by lack of practice.

The man remembered a boyhood promise to himself. It would be different when he grew up. He was not going to live a life of 'just making ends meet', of 'keeping up appearances' and 'endlessly moving from pillar to post'. Yet, even though his lifestyle and environment had improved relative to those of his parents, he had still been influenced by others. He had even caught himself saying the same things to his children, as his parents had said to him. The very things that he had sworn never to do. In retrospect, he realised that his parents had done the best they could. But had he?

He began to consider that, if he had chosen this environment—even his parents—then it was certainly not conducive to learning. Not only had he not learned, it seemed to him that he had merely become an extension of his environment, living with the same frustrations with which his parents had lived. He had actually enjoyed some good times—happy times—but, generally, his life had seemed to be one of mere existence. He now recognised that he had never really been in control of his life. It was a world of mislaid dreams, lost hope; a world of being controlled.

*

"Why did I choose that life?" he spoke aloud.

"Life is not about how you suppose it should be, it just is", the voice began. "It is the way that you choose to cope with it, which makes the difference. Your spirit selected the parents who would offer the best chance of providing the lessons it wished to learn. By physical manifestation you were given a certain pattern of energies which would attract the people and circumstances necessary for certain experiences.

"Everyone learns from experiences, particularly the difficult and uncomfortable ones—where the physical heart weeps, the spiritual soul laughs. Because your spirit accepts that there is a reason behind every experience. In realisation this life becomes easier.

"There is no such thing as a wasted life, good, or bad luck. Your spirit, which is pure potential, seeks to evolve into a great spirit of love and wisdom, in order that it can become part of the perfect expression of these qualities—God. Its evolution and wisdom is gained through existence on the physical plane.

"Although your spirit has the free will to choose the life it seeks, its physical form is subject to a programming, which often causes a wrong decision to be made, when a pre-arranged challenge is met. In your physical form you are not aware of what you have come to do, because that knowledge could prevent the challenges being met.

"This is how you can be diverted from your course, failing to learn or achieve that which is intended. You are not without a specific mission or learning purpose, no one is and, as such, no one is in your life by accident. Each person is in your life as a blessing not a punishment, although this is not immediately perceived.

"Human relationships are part of why we live, as only through them can we grow and awaken. Some people offer major lessons, others minor. You were to offer your parents lessons, as much as they were to provide you with lessons. Love, tolerance, understanding and acceptance."

"But we seemed to all love each other," the man said, "my mother certainly provided loving and happy times. I can't understand why our lives were filled with so much desperation, anxiety and bickering?"

The man knew his words reflected the sadness he was feeling because the voice became softer. He felt its kindness coming to him.

"Quite simply because we use emotionally backed desires to secure our happiness. This is the way we are taught to be happy but it doesn't work. It may bring temporary feelings of pleasure, which provide the motivation for the action, but it does not bring happiness."

"What do you mean by emotionally backed desires?" questioned the man.

"In order to achieve perfect expression with the qualities of The Infinite Spirit, God, each spirit sets out for a specific purpose. Within every specific purpose there is a fundamental quest. This immensely challenging quest is to learn to love unconditionally. Your family had no knowledge of the enjoyment of unconditional love and therefore no experience to express it.

"The physical body assumes, because of programming in its first few years of life, that its desires, which are the result of its emotional feelings, are the true guides to doing the things that will make it happy. No one will ever find happiness or fulfilment through emotionally backed desires because they are, in effect, conditionally based. These conditionally based desires in seeking to be satisfied lead us from one illusion of happiness to another. It is the delusion of: 'if I could just do this, or that, then I will be happy'."

The man remembered how often both his parents had said something similar.

*

"*If I could just earn more money then I'd be happy*", his father was always saying that to his mother, "*I could take us on holiday, buy the family some new clothes.*" He would tighten his tie, studying himself in the hall mirror and then announce, "*But I'm not going to get it where I am now—it's like a dead end.*"

At that point they would all realise that they would soon be packing and beginning again, things were to be changed by a change of address. The finish of this familiar speech was usually something along the lines of, "*If I could get the promotion I'm due I'd be a lot happier, it would mean moving but I know you'd be happier in a nice new house, somewhere different.*" He would then beam approvingly at them all and leave for work.

Many memories assured him that, despite several actual moves, promotions and changing jobs, the refrains had continued. He thought of how often he, himself, had used them. He had also eventually borrowed the later one of, *"If I could only find the right person to love, then I would be happy."*

\*

"Emotionally backed desires guide us in our relationships", the voice continued, in an uncanny invasion of the man's thoughts, "so we search for someone whom we believe is the right person to fit our needs and desires. There are pleasurable times, but as we love conditionally, which is control based love, the relationship deteriorates and we convince ourselves it wasn't the right person after all.

"Those who follow the intended path of learning unconditional love know that it is more important to *be* the right person, than to *find* the right person. All unpleasant emotions are absolutely unnecessary and are misleading guides to effective actions in our lives. Yet, most people continually beat themselves up, mentally, when the outside world does not conform with the emotional conditioning of their inside world.

"Their very actions keep them on the roller coaster ride, which maintains their presence in the lower levels of consciousness. The spirit is desperately seeking to raise itself from these levels, but hits the difficulty that almost every way we were taught to work towards happiness actually leads us away from it."

"Almost every way we were taught to work towards happiness has the opposite effect?" The man registered surprise but quickly felt another, far stronger emotion replace it. "But if that is the case," he began tentatively, "then the action, my action, was hardly my fault." He paused, seeking confirmation that he was, after all, blameless for what had actually been beyond his control.

"Accepting and shifting responsibilities cannot be dispensed with so simply", the voice was firm.

"I was not seeking justification." Here the man stopped, because both he, and the voice, knew that he was. He paused while he considered, again, the enormity of what the voice had previously said, then questioned, "Why were we taught this way?"

"We have allowed our true self to be compromised without being aware of it, that is the short answer", the voice returned.

There was a lengthy silence while the man waited, eager for it to continue. This voice, with its patient determination, was giving him reason, knowledge, and something equally as valuable, time. Time to talk. Time to listen.

"Most of mankind occupies a level of consciousness which seeks expression through control," the voice began again, its undulations pleasantly taking the words and carrying them in to the man's mind.

"This control is sought through a misguided belief that it will provide the security which is continually craved: it is a delusion; a delusion created by our outside world. Each of us lives in two worlds at the same time. An outer and an inner world. Both have paths to human advancement, the urge for acquisition and power, and the drive to self transcendence.

"People live in an outer physical world which comprises of other people, money, material possessions, cars, homes and governments. They dwell, also, in an inner, spiritual world of thoughts, feelings, intuition and desires. Both are necessary to develop the balance important to raise your consciousness but although the primary teaching of the ancients was to place your inner world first, the mass of mankind chose not to.

"Thus it is with the biblical story of Cain and Abel. Each brother illustrates the two options available in the quest to learn in the physical world.

"Cain is characterised by the motivation to *acquire*, which is the Hebrew derivative of his name. He represents an option which perceives objects as separate things to be acquired, controlled and manipulated. Egotistically driven this world is seen as 'how does this effect me?' and 'how can I make use of it?'"

As he listened the man felt guilty and thought how he had gauged so much of what he had done, even for others, on exactly that measurement.

"Where Cain is the *grasping* option, Abel represents the *receptive* option which, associated with a moderate ego, perceives his world as an interrelated whole. Abel is derived from the Hebrew root, meaning *breath,* which is symbolic of how the mind is made still, and listened to, through meditation. As the external grasping quality of mind diminishes, the inner receptive mind begins to know itself and remember its purpose.

"The continual struggle between these two options, mankind's two worlds, is illustrated in all true religions. The stories further symbolise how civilisation for centuries has been dominated by the Cain option which had overpowered the Abel option.

"This thinking forms the foundation for how people treat others. Man generally seeks to derive his security and happiness through manipulation and control of his external world. This world he considers to be separate from himself.

"The truth is that man's inner world controls and determines his outer. Because mankind does not realise or accept this truth, however, it continues to always feel insecure and unhappy."

The man remembered how he had tried, continually, to organise his life to derive the greatest satisfaction. Whatever satisfaction he did attain never quite seemed to last long, however. It never quite delivered the security, or happiness for that matter, that he had hoped it would.

"Almost in every way we express ourselves in the Cain mode," the voice continued. "Your parents unwittingly instilled a form of thinking in you, in the first few years of your life, in the same way that they were emotionally programmed, unwittingly, by their parents.

"Their actions *overpowered* your inner world causing it to become submissive to your outer world. The outer world dictates, so, to accommodate it, to survive, we developed a consciousness which focused on emotionally intense programmes of security, pleasure and control. We learned to control and manipulate others through conditional love.

"Imagine you had to decide between two choices of life available to you. One keeps you happy, only where things turn out the way you desired and hoped for, and the other choice keeps you happy, no matter what happens. Which one would you choose?"

"The second one," the man answered unhesitatingly.

"Of course. Amazingly, however, the majority of people choose the first because they have been instilled with false ideas of what *will* make them happy. They grow up thinking, wrongly, that happiness is theirs when they get what they want. What they actually feel is a thrill, ego-satisfaction or sense of power—none of which is happiness."

The man thought about all those things that he had so craved. Yet, if he was honest, the happiness he had felt on receiving them had been empty. It had not lasted and he had soon resorted to needing something better. "Why do we think that we derive happiness in this way?"

"Because of the dominant negative emotions developed in response to seeking some form of guide to actions in life. They were developed when, for example, you experienced, your mother forcibly removing something, which you were not allowed, from your small hands, while at the same time sending out bad vibrations based on her desire not to have the object broken. You cried and registered the first of many admonitions on how the world should be, or how you should act.

"You developed a self consciousness, in order to protect yourself, and an acute awareness to anyone's actions or vibrations, which you believed threatened your ability to control and manipulate people and things around you. You developed an ego, which needed to perceive continually greater external evidence of its position, in order to feel secure.

"This false sense of security, however, is never satiated because it relies on external gratification. You were born with the basic capacity for perceiving the world very clearly. But the conditioned, false you, developed in your formative years, developed a different guide to handle and view the world, that actually anchored you to the three lower levels of consciousness.

"These lower levels will always divert you from the reality of your life, which is to live in the present moment. Instead it forces you to spend your life continually wishing that any present moment was a better situation for you. This in turn lowers your perceptiveness and keeps you from eliminating the frustration that you allow to grow from your circumstances and problems.

"False ideas about how you believe life *should* be for you build on top of each other. At the time you are not aware they are false, because you are not your *true* internally driven *self*. You become a conditional, *externally influenced self*. Anyone who is not their self, cannot be at peace with their self. They have to know who they are. How can you be at peace if you do not understand who you are?"

The man remained silent and listened for the voice. He became aware of a light which seemed to reflect on part of him. His mind went back to a bedroom where he would lie in his bed gazing at the light which shone from the full moon. He had been told that the moon's light was not its own—it was a reflection—borrowed light from the sun.

Perhaps that's why it always seemed to him to be artificial—not day or night, not black or white. He had been like that, always reflecting back to people what he thought they wanted from him, or, more often, reflecting a facade in order to get from them what he wanted.

He considered the voice's last words and decided that he had never really been himself, in fact he probably wouldn't have recognised it if he had been. He had always tried to be so many different things to many different people. He had to be—he had always felt so shy, so self-conscious. No, he thought, not always—not as a very young child—it was only later he had started to feel insecure. When had he started feeling insecure?

He had a sense that it was when he was unable to get his own way. In fact, it seemed to him he got what he wanted less and less. He had believed that people had purposely prevented him from getting what he had set out to do. He felt the familiar feeling of frustration build up. It was curiously comforting—something into which he could retreat, when the world misunderstood him.

•

*"Why didn't they choose me?"* he saw himself asking his mother, his face twisted, his words high pitched and peevish.

*"Choose you for what?"* Her indifference was obvious, probably even to an extremely angry little boy.

Why was it she never listened to him, the way she did to the others, really listened in a way that made him feel important?

*"I told you, for the school play, for the leading part, the one that I practised for, the one I can do! Instead, I am just one of the people who walk about and say nothing. It's not fair. I never get to speak!"*

*"Perhaps they felt another boy should have the opportunity to do it?"*

*"Oh yes, another boy gets the opportunity—it is always someone else—never me. I think they leave me out on purpose, that's what I think!"*

The school bag was banged down on to the kitchen table. It knocked the milk jug slightly so that it spilled droplets of milk onto one of his books. His mother sighed mildly, mopped them up, and tried to placate him with *"Well, perhaps they thought rehearsals were difficult for you, because you live further from the school than most of the others"*

He was just considering an acceptance of this token excuse, when she wrecked everything by adding *"although your sister was in it last year."* He knew that he was fighting back the tears as he rushed out of the kitchen and threw *"It's no good talking to you—you don't understand"* back at her.

Then the scenario broke up but he knew that she would have shouted something up the stairs at him. Probably, something along the lines of *"You come back here right now, ...getting just like your father, ...upset when you don't get your own way."* He was certain that the exchange would have ended with the words *"I won't be spoken to like that, particularly when I don't deserve it! After all I do for you..."* this was her instinctive last resort to finish him off.

His thoughts settled on the reference to his father. It was odd how she had begun to compare him to his father, after the divorce. Interestingly, it seemed that all the bad things about him were inherited from the paternal side, and the few good points that he possessed came from her. Divorce. Irretrievable breakdown. He had looked the words up because no one would tell him what they meant. None the wiser, he had asked around at school.

No one could exactly explain 'irretrievable'—but they did say that since his father was living with someone else, now, it was unlikely that his mother would take him back. It appeared that no-one's mother seemed to understand how a father could do that.

He knew his parents were always saying that they did

not understand each other, and that was before the divorce. So there had seemed little hope now.

It occurred to him that he couldn't think of any people he knew, who had seemed to understand each other, or had appeared to take the time to try. Yet, oddly enough, everyone he knew was always making comparisons and sitting in judgement on each other. He did it himself, he recognised this.

His feelings about other people were based on how he thought they ought to be and what he thought they should do. And, most of his conversations were about justifying these thoughts and opinions. Maybe his ideas were false of how life should be. Surely, even though he may not have been always right, seldom had he been wrong?

Now he began to feel a little uneasy at the way his mind was working. If, as the voice had said, we are not aware that our ideas are false, because we are false and when we are not ourselves, we are not at peace then, surely, he had never been at peace with himself?

Clearly, he had always been searching for something, but he had never discovered precisely what it was. At times he had felt so definite about something, then, later, he was never so certain. For most of his life he had either compared himself with what others wanted, or had been compared with what others wanted. Confusion was creating questions and panic began to pervade his reasoning. Where was the voice?

*

"I need to know, can you tell me this? Can anyone ever understand who they really are?"

"There are many different roles in life which make up the *'I'* of an individual," the voice answered at once, "all of which operate under different guises of self-consciousness. The true self, which is complete unity, has no need for shyness. It has no need to impress, it simply expresses. That which you call *yourself* is not you. You are not your body, not your race nor culture, you are not your intellect nor your emotions, you are not brain nor your name.

"You are Divine Spirit, Pure Potential, yet your conditioned mind does not want its false security threatened by your *true unified self.* So, to prevent you knowing yourself, it has developed a make-up of numerous *'I's.* Each time you think *'I'* this is later overridden by a different *'I'* which, in turn, has no dominion over the next *'I'.*

"The *I* that declares that you will rise early in the morning is not the same *I* that exists in the morning and, as such, refuses to co-operate. Each *I,* so far as *a disunited self* is concerned, is in command. With such a host of 'Generals' is it any wonder that most people lose the battle of understanding who they are?"

The man thought about how often he had changed his mind about things, particularly people. His opinions had been chameleon-like, created to suit the situation.

"The *I* who decides to take time to consider what is really important in your life promises to start that very evening. The 'evening' *I*, however, may take another view. This one will consider that the subject of personal evaluation is far too important to do now, so chooses to defer the task until the week-end. In turn, the 'week-end' *I*, to which the task has been delegated, has other plans. After all, how can you spend a well-deserved break-time doing something that is so important?

"This *I* easily delegates to the future *I*, that will be in command on your holiday. It is of no concern to each *I* what has been previously decided when it takes 'office', as former *I* 'governments' have no jurisdiction."

The man swiftly considered the many times that he had been unable to keep promises, even those which he had made to himself. Especially those particularly important ones concerning what he had wanted to do, that had just not been followed through. He had not got down to doing it. It was so very laborious evaluating yourself. It was much easier, and he'd believed just as effective, to ask others what *they* thought he should do. He, in turn, had readily advised others when they had asked the same of him.

"Would you expect that with all of these different '*I*'s," the voice said, "it is possible to be sincere with oneself? Because sincerity cannot grow when there is so much disunity, the answer can only be no.

"If you cannot be sincere with yourself, how is it possible to be sincere with others? It is not. Therefore, the tendency is to be judgmental towards others, which is the outgrowth of disunity developed by your conditioned mind. When you are in a unified state of mind, then you are being *true* to yourself. This is a level of consciousness that neither requires justification, nor to seek to justify it. At this level, you have the courage of your convictions.

"This level of consciousness can only be attained by knowing who you are, which is certainly possible, but only through working on yourself. This is not easy but you do have that dynamic of your spirit that can help to guide you. People make it difficult for themselves simply because they refuse to ever listen to this guide.

"The constant dialogue of others, who, in their own particular judgmental way, *know best*, combines with the loud chatter of the argumentative 'I's, which our conditioned mind allows inside our head, and therefore completely drowns this voice.

"On the rare occasion, when it does manage to make itself heard, it is not recognised and its valuable message is dismissed as an absurdity."

The man felt even further disquieted. He was aware that there had been several 'important' occasions in his life when his first, second and third thoughts had confused him to the point where he could not make a decision. Any final decision he had reached was frequently attained following the bouncing of his various options off other people, and then catching the one thrown back to him as being the best.

Looking back, now, he was aware that he had taken the easiest way out of everything. He had steadily avoided seduction by any softly sounding, inner voice of his own. Experience had provided him with regrets for doing so. But, he comforted himself with the knowledge, at that time, he had not felt comfortable going against the suggestions of those with whom he had discussed things, particularly his family. A family who taught each other to believe that it was wrong to put yourself first, you had to think of others. It was not right to please yourself.

Yet, these borrowed decisions, which were considered

to be best, according to the people meant to be the nearest to him, had held him back from doing what he had really sensed he should do at the time. Surely, if he had put himself first he would have got it right, whatever *it* was meant to be. Then he, along with everyone else, would have grown?

"To have the courage of your own convictions. That's what you are getting at. To live the life you're intended to live, making your own decisions about who you are, and what you will become. Not passively submitting to what others think is best for you? Following your own heart." His words sounded bitter but this was smothered, slowly, by the stronger emotion of sorrow.

"Why is it so difficult to just be *yourself* and why did I spend my life pleasing others—does everybody? Is that the way it has to be? Surely, if the simplest answer is to *know* yourself, why is it so hard to do? I always believed that I was being me. I may have been judgmental towards others but isn't everyone? How else can you advise them? What was I to do?"

The barrage of questions that the man fired at the voice seem to bombard his own head. But, he fought like a soldier trapped in a trench of unknowns. Then, with the courage that comes from desperation, he began to scrutinise the picture appearing before him.

*

*"Well she would say that wouldn't she?"* his friend retorted. *"What do you expect? I'd watch it if I were you, or she will finish with you. The trouble with you is you're too serious."*

The young man outwardly shrugged his shoulders and hurled an imaginary missile at the world. Inwardly, he began to wrestle with the panic and the antagonism. Panic, because this wasn't what he had wanted to hear, he didn't want to be finished with. Antagonism, because what his friend had said made sense, and it always seemed to. They often walked home from school together sharing their news. Today, his had been the earlier conversation that had taken place with his new girlfriend.

*"Oh no I'm not!"*

*"Oh yes you are!"* His friend returned in the best pantomime spirit, but then added in a more thoughtful tone, *"Yes, definitely too intense."*

*"But you told me last week that I should be serious with her. To tell her that if she really liked me she wouldn't talk to other boys the way she does."*

He had followed this advice and was now being

accused, by her, of being too possessive!

*"That's what you'd do, you said, show her who's boss. Now you tell me what do I expect! Some friend you are,"* he added, *"I reckon you fancy her yourself and this is all part of a plan to go out with her."*

*"That's stupid!"* his friend's voice rose in defence. *"I don't like her at all, and wouldn't go out with her if you paid me. Look at the crowd she hangs around with. She's just trying to show them how she can control all the boys she goes out with. She's on a power trip and you're just a pawn in her game, not mine."*

The young man was livid with his friend, for, yet again, what he said seemed to make sense. He was dismally aware that he had no clear idea of what to do. He didn't want to finish with her—he couldn't—yet her actions really annoyed him. Why couldn't she feel the same way he did? If she would only get jealous when he looked at someone else he knew he'd feel more secure, but she never did.

He even tried talking about his few previous girlfriends to which she had responded with a formidable list of former boyfriends. He couldn't stand it! She *was* in control of him. In fact, she was in control of herself. That's how she had attracted him a few weeks before—she had known exactly what she was doing. Then, just when he had shown his feelings, she didn't seem to be interested anymore.

*"What should I do?"* he demanded, but his friend had gone.

*

The man had observed the scene. Saw how he had acted, never confident of making his own decisions. Always seeking to justify his actions. Part of that justification seemed to include being judgmental about people, particularly those whom he believed had hurt him.

"Only you have the power to make yourself unhappy," he heard the voice say to him. "It is not the actions of others that have the ultimate control over you, it is how you perceive those actions. So, whenever you react to someone you are giving them control over you. Conversely, whenever you respond you control yourself. It's your choice."

"I wasn't aware there was even a difference, let alone a choice," said the man. "Is that because I didn't know the *true* me of which you spoke?"

"Mankind is only unique in nature *because* of his power of choice, which is just as well because there is *always* a choice. You do not, however, have power over consequence. Whether you choose to be the *real* you or the *conditioned,* you will inevitably effect the consequence of your life. This is one of Life's immutable Laws which operates even though you are ignorant of it."

"My whole life was lived on the conditioned me, wasn't it?"

"Your conditioned mind is constantly effected by the circumstances that you, and all your different rôles, played by different I's, find themselves", confirmed the voice. "Unaware that you have manifested your external world you seek to control, manipulate and organise situations to feel secure. Consequently your actions are re-actions which you see as having to be taken in order to keep the external world from destroying you.

"On occasions when everything was going well, just the way you wanted it, you did not believe that it would last because *something* beyond your control would spoil it. Consequently in your relationships, with others, you would be more aware of those weaker aspects, which threatened your false sense of security, and would react accordingly for reassurance.

"You took actions to ensure your status quo against the external world—a position that you believed to be just keeping ahead of it—but they did not develop the limitless potential caged inside you. For example, regardless of how

much you earned during your life, and it was always more
and more, it was never quite enough, was it?"

*"It was not the amount I was hoping for, but it is the figure I was expecting"*, his mother and sister had been listening, as he told them how his interview had concluded, with him being employed.

*"It's enough to get by on,"* replied his sister, *"at least you're lucky to have got the job so quickly. I had to wait ages before I found anything."*

*"Yes, I know that, but I'm not sure whether it's what I want to do."*

His mother, who looked worn out by her latest part-time job, joined in, *"You don't seem to be satisfied whatever you get! If you are asking me the hours are regular and it's very convenient"* her eyes challenged him to dispute these facts and then she continued, *"which is more than you can say for mine. Anyway, it will be good experience for you."*

*"Yes, I know that too,"* he had agreed, *"both the career adviser and the interviewer said it was a good start for*

*someone in my position, and it offers good advancement, if I keep at it and work hard. It's just not what I want to do, although if the money was better I wouldn't mind so much."*

His mother reinforced her opinion with, *"Well, at least it provides security, which is the main thing. It is a good start, as they said, and you have to start somewhere"*, but then added, *"What did they mean, someone in your position?"*

*"I don't know, someone with my limited qualifications, I think he said."*

*"And whose fault is that?"* his mothers' voice had raised slightly. *"It's certainly not mine!"* Then it got higher, *"Why, I gave you..."*

*"I'm not saying that it is your fault,"* interrupted the man, stressing the 'not'. *"If anything it was the teachers. They never seemed to have the time to teach. They were too busy telling us what a waste of time we all were. Anyway I'm not complaining. I'm pleased about the job, of course I am. It's just..."*

*"... Not what you want to do!"* his sister's voice, finishing what he was going to say. *"That's all you ever say"* she continued. *"Well, I don't know about Mum, but I'm dying to know what this wonderful thing is that you want to do? That's if you know!"*

That was just it, the man realised, he hadn't known. But he had felt *sure* that he would have recognised what he had wanted, once he had found it.

*

"If you don't know where you are going," he felt the voice climbing back into his thoughts, "how will you know when you get there?"

The man wanted to push it away again. "Listen, something always turns up that you *hope* will be right for you, and, at that time, surely you'd just know it was right."

"Hope is important, for, without it, Life's dream would be empty", replied the voice. "It is the intangible element which promises to keep you going through all difficulties, but it lacks power if there is not a purpose or goal to motivate it. Your hopes and imagination are closely linked and are both at your disposal to develop your dreams.

"Sadly too many people use them *for* the disposal of their dreams. Where your hopes of expectation are founded in a solid belief in your self-worth, they are strong. Yet when your hopes are founded on merely wishing for things to improve, they are weak."

The man remembered how often he had wished that

he could improve his lot. Most mornings, looking in the mirror while shaving, he had hoped something would go really well for him at work, that he would at least receive some praise, but he'd never really *expected* it.

*

"*Expect the worst and hope for the best, that's my motto*", his Uncle always used to dole out advice at family gatherings. He was his father's elder brother and had a whole repertoire of similar sayings.

The trouble was that if he was honest with himself he had to admit that he had usually agreed with their sentiment. 'Why was it that everyone always spoke in clichés while handing out advice?', he thought. Where had they all come from? It was certainly not in agreement with what he was hearing now.

There had been moments in his life when he had experienced very high expectations and someone would say, 'Don't expect too much of yourself' or 'Don't raise your hopes too much.' He couldn't help but lower his expectations, which was just as well as he had only just met them.

*

"One of our greatest gifts," continued the voice, "our imagination, is so adversely affected by our conditioned beliefs that it restricts our growth like a ruthless dictator. It almost forces us to keep our mind on what we *don't* want to happen rather than what we *do* want to happen. Our expectations obligingly adjust themselves accordingly. In turn another of our gifts, our natural desire, is stunted and utilised more to survive than grow, to get by, rather than to get on."

"Desire is a gift?" questioned the man in amazement. "But I believed that you shouldn't really have desires, that they were sinful, that they should be controlled."

"Desire actually means 'of the father', it is God's gift to ensure that you are *able* to grow into everything that is intended for you. Without desire you could not grow, it is the starting point of all achievement. Yet this has not stopped most religions trying to renounce it. But there is nothing shameful in wanting to have wealth and material possessions. It is when these *external* things are looked upon to *fulfil* our spiritual needs, which is something they cannot do, that life becomes a dilemma."

"There were times," the man said quietly, "when I felt ashamed for wanting so much. I thought I didn't deserve it, that it wasn't my lot in life to have what I wanted. Once, I even thought that maybe God didn't want me to have it, because I was always wanting *so much*."

"God's ability to give to you is only limited by your own ability to receive", the voice replied. "The strength of your desire is a measure of your willingness to *receive* what God wants to give. An inner turmoil arises from the struggles and judgement you experience when your conditioned beliefs build barriers to block your desires."

"By making you feel guilty about even having them?"

The man knew all about the guilt that followed desire. The strongest longing he had ever felt in his life was to buy himself a cottage in the countryside. He had spent months searching for exactly the right position. It was everything he had ever imagined possible for his perfect home.

After that came the wishing, striving, working, the desperate hope that the mortgage would come through. Then, when close to completing on it, he had driven over to take a final look before it became his. Sitting in his car he had enjoyed the beauty of it, the feeling of pleasure it was giving him to know that it would soon belong to him.

Then niggling thoughts, twinges of uncertainty, began making their way into his plans. He slowly allowed himself to be overwhelmed by a feeling of unworthiness. 'Why do I *deserve* to have this? None of my family have ever lived anywhere as lovely as this. There are other people who merit this more. His mother had worked so hard all her life, surely she deserved this more than he did?' Then having talked himself out of it, it had never happened anyway. Something had delayed the mortgage going through and he had lost it to another, more definite buyer.

"Yes," he sighed aloud, "Guilt certainly blocks desires, but sometimes isn't it necessary for some desires to go unattained?"

"It is important to interpret how and why they should be achieved," the voice assented. "It is how most people struggle over obtaining what they desire: to have their own way, to grab, to hold, or possess, that causes them such pain. Attachment is given to their achievements, possessions or status in the false belief that it will give fulfilment.

"Your spirit, which dwells in your inner world, understands that desire is simply a path towards fulfilment. It does not attach itself to the external gratification desired by its initial levels of consciousness, because it knows that the path continues beyond this. Your spirit accepts that it must first pass through the desires of seeking security, pleasure and control before it can experience the desires of unity, awareness and beyond.

"Your conditioned mind, however, does not like

accepting non-attachment to those external elements, which it views as vital to its security, pleasure and control. So it will keep you searching for fulfilment in more possessions and money; the need for attention through sex, or making your presence felt, or power through status, position and control. "Attachment to these expressions of desire can become increasingly unhealthy as life's history illustrates.

"It is important to understand the nature of your desires and to recognise that all of them are intended to come true, which is why you have them. You would not have had them if you had not been given the ability to achieve them. If you believe that you don't deserve them, then your self-judgement will prevent them achieving their natural course.

"God has already given the gift of an abundant world, that is full of opportunity, and wants to grant your desires in order that you can grow. Imagine that every one of your desires has a spiritual meaning and provides another step on your path to being the best you can be.

"Your hopes, expectations, and desires must not be allowed to be distorted by a fearful imagination which holds you back from fulfilling your potential. Yet when we do not think for ourselves, and allow others to do our thinking for us, this is exactly what happens. We become increasingly unsure of ourselves, of what we want to *be* and *become*. We think only of what we want to *do* and *have* and imagine the awful insecurity that we fear will happen if we are unable to have what we want."

The man remembered always feeling insecure if he did not attain what he had been striving for. He was more concerned at what others would think of him. So, he had to look good, drive a decent car, have a good job and hold an important position.

He had even lied to create the required impression.

*

*"Oh hi Dad!" He said as he picked up the 'phone.*

*"Hi son, how've you been, and how's that new job promotion you told me about ?"*

*"Oh, I mentioned that did I? Well it's..."*

*"I knew you'd get it! You see, even though I wasn't there to advise you as much as I would have liked, you've still done well. I'm so proud of you. Tell me, does it include that executive car and all those perks you were looking forward to?"*

*"Well the details are still being sorted out. But look Dad, I can't talk right now... I've got to go, I'm due at a meeting."*

*"O.K., O.K., I know busy exec now eh? But give us a call when you can. Hey, maybe we could meet for one of those super lunches you're always arranging and have a proper chat?"*

*"Yes Dad, that'll be nice... I'll give you a call. Bye."*

•

Because of his weakness he lived beyond his means. Rather than spend his time thinking *how* he could change the situation, it seemed to him now that he had spent his whole time worrying about what would happen to him if he was unable to meet his bills, or pay his mortgage.

His imagination had indeed developed desires of survival. His expectation had been one of getting by, *never* of getting on. Where he had believed he was working in his best interests, he had actually been working against them!

"Why did I allow my imagination to work against me?"

"That part of you which seeks security through attachment to an external reality is your ego," returned the voice. "Your imagination rules your world and you allowed your ego full control over it. So, with your ego in command of your thoughts, you gave it full rein to your feelings and actions."

"But wasn't my ego me anyway?" the man asked.

"It was a conscious thinking part of you, yes. But it viewed itself as a part that must increasingly protect itself. It did this by attaching itself to those thoughts which it believed would bring it a sense of importance."

"What do you mean by *attaches* itself?"

"Everyone has countless thoughts each day. All of them are of no consequence unless meaning is attached to them. This is done by not letting the thought drift by. The more something is dwelt on, the more meaning it is given. Greater meaning develops greater importance to the point that, whatever it is, must be done or acquired, or the ego feels threatened.

"This insecurity will cause you to put all your energies into getting that, which, is now viewed, as really *important*. It may be someone's comment that you feel threatens your talent, skill, position, or standing. It could be how you view yourself. It may be your need to have a better car, house, clothes or holiday in order to illustrate to others that you are doing well.

"True success in life begins with the subordination of the ego. This happens when you *let go* of the concern of doing things to impress others, and you do whatever you do, because you have chosen to. When your decisions pander to your ego's misguided thoughts of security, it may *seem* that they are in your best interests. They may be in the short term, but, in the long term, you work *against* yourself."

The man recalled how many of his actions had been made with the thought of 'how good he would look in the eyes of others'. It was important to him what people thought of him and, particularly as a younger man, he had always wanted to stand out from the crowd. He could recall how he had felt about getting that long awaited promotion in the firm.

•

Driving home in the new car, radio blaring, windows open, sun beating down on the unblemished bonnet. Waving to some of the office girls as he left the car park. Shouting out the usual *"Bye, have a good weekend, see you Monday!"*, but soaking up the admiring looks he had received from a couple of them. Relishing the envious looks that he had got from a couple of the men in his division. Yes! He had done it! He had worked with this in mind and now he had proved it to himself and others! He had sung along with the music at the top of his voice. No longer just an ordinary person, but different, successful and he was showing the world.

Then, he remembered stopping to give a friend a lift home. At first it had given him a real high to have company in his special moment. Slowly, after expressing his gratitude for the unexpected lift, this drinking pal and so-called mate, managed to point out that it was only a firm's car, and not even a deluxe model at that.

*"They can't think that much of you,"* he easily quipped. *"It's probably in line with some of the redundancies being made at your place at the moment—you'd better enjoy it while you can!"*

He had smiled and pretended take the teasing banter in his stride, but inwardly, there it was again, the panic! He knew his friend didn't mean it. But he could not stop himself seeing the risk. No, he tried to reassure himself, after dropping his friend home, he wasn't going to lose it. There was no reason to, he had worked hard for it. But his friend had a point. Why hadn't he been given a deluxe. His colleague had been given one and he really hadn't been there any longer than him.

By the time he had walked into his house he was full of resentment; considering the fact that perhaps they had not thought so much of him after all. Perhaps those looks, when he'd left, were really mock admiration from those girls, even amusement from the men. Had they been mocking and laughing at him. Surely not?

He remembered that this resentment had continued for some time until, one afternoon, the operations manager had asked him what the problem was. It was only the manager's patience and skill that had finally got him to admit why he was feeling the way he was.

When he had admitted that he felt discriminated against, because his colleague had been awarded the superior car, he remembered how the manager had replied in surprise, *"But you could have had one as well. Didn't you know that you could choose to put in some of your own money for a deluxe model? Your colleague chose to because he has a family."*

The embarrassment had been painful but was swiftly overcome by his anger that no-one had thought to inform him about the option.

The man now recognised that he had been inflicting the hurt upon himself. It was his hurt ego that had made him feel so insecure. All the pain he had felt over something, that should have given him immense pleasure, was down to him. His imagination at that time had run riot for weeks, always thinking the worst.

\*

"Your ego is not aware that it is being detrimental to you, moreover it believes it is protecting you," he heard the voice once more break into his thoughts.

"But surely it's your own worst enemy?" the man demanded in exasperation.

"Only when misuse allows it to get above itself, as to put it. When you become aware of it and you are able to recognise its false demands it can then used as an ally rather than a foe."

"But how can you become aware of it when it seems to have so much control?"

The voice waited.

*"I'm sorry but with the way everything is at the moment some drastic measures need to be taken."*

The man was stunned. Redundancy? His mind had stopped listening to all the excuses—he didn't care. His thoughts were filled with the horror and the hell of what he was going to do. How was he going to tell his fiancée? What would his family and friends think? What would he do for money? My God, what about the new house? Their joint incomes were needed for the mortgage! His horror turned to anger. A huge and hopeless anger, that he directed at his manager, who had just given him the news.

*"This isn't fair!"* He knew he was shouting, and that colleagues would hear him, but that was beyond his control. *"You promised me good future prospects if I worked hard. Well I have! Really hard. For five bloody years and for what? Nothing but an 'I'm sorry'. Well, sorry isn't going to cover my commitments is it?"*

*"You have more than that"*, began the manager, looking miserable from spending a whole day at having to do something that had made him sick to the stomach. Obviously feeling helpless because all he could do was attempt to console these people, some with whom he had worked closely for many years.

*"You have your experience, and you have been well trained for what you do. Also, there will be some redundancy money which will help. And of course, the company has arranged for you to be given advice on finding another position and you will receive a good reference."*

The man remembered the way that his anger abandoned him, leaving him to plead if there was anything he could do. But he knew nothing would, or could, be forthcoming and his anger soon returned, when he realised that he would even lose his transport at the end of that month.

After four weeks of non-productive interviews he had lost what little confidence he had left. He had grown gaunt faced and exhausted from trying to hide the fact that everything wasn't all right. He'd began to hate the inevitable questions which others always seem to raise in conversation.

At first when people asked what he did he would answer that he had just been roughly treated, unfairly made redundant and was currently engaged in seeking other opportunities. People had been supportive at first. Agreeing how unfair it was. Full of suggestions about what he should, or should not do.

After a while this had progressed to embarrassment when they heard that he was still redundant. Then came the pity. He imagined that people were beginning to dodge him, wanting to avoid the risk of catching this redundancy thing that he had.

Another trial was having to travel by public transport to every interview. He had felt humiliated, particularly when he had to seek support from social security for his mortgage payments.

Yes, the man thought, his ego had certainly taken a knock during that period of his life. His only thoughts were of getting back everything that had been unfairly taken away from him. He had felt afraid, insecure and lost. At times he almost resented everyone, with their jobs and their pitying looks.

He had taken offence when one well meaning individual had asked him, *"What is it you would really like to do?"* and then suggested that this could be an ideal opportunity to do something different, as *"Now is the time to take advantage of the situation into which you have been placed."*

At the time he had replied that it was easy to say something like that when you have your business, as he knew the person had, but what did he know about being redundant?

But later, half watching the television at home he had chewed over the fact that there could be a lot of sense in this comment. Perhaps he ought to take the opportunity to re-evaluate his life and consider what he really wanted to do?

•

"Even when I was experiencing adversity I don't believe that I was aware of my ego controlling me," he began to tell the voice. "I was only concerned with how I was going to cope in the future. I had the opportunity to make new plans but I could not get my mind off how cheated I felt. How I had to get back what I'd lost. That was all I could think of at the time. If this was my ego, as you say, causing my hurt, what should I have done differently to have been able to control it?"

"By being conscious of the *present* moment," answered the voice. "Your ego prefers to live in the future, or the past, rather than the present. It likes nothing better, for example, than to reminisce about how the good old days were or about how it has suffered. It fantasises about how everything will be better next year, and how it's going to be. When all your energy is used up doing this, there is no energy to live in the present moment, which is where your life is."

"But if being conscious means being aware, I'm sure I was conscious of what I was doing at any particular time."

"Most people are not aware that they are even being unaware", the voice said. "Preoccupied with worrying about the future, or feeling guilty about the past, they spend most of their lives being somewhere they are not. Feeling guilty about not being home, when working late at the office, and worrying about finishing a report, while at home, is not living in the here and now."

The man considered later times in his life. Those countless week-ends when he had taken his own family on outings, but he had not really been with them. He was there but his mind was on other things. There had been pressing matters that he had to resolve at work and found it difficult to take his mind off them.

He thought of one evening at which time he couldn't remember a particular occasion that his children had been talking about. He had argued with them and was certain he had not been there.

*"But Dad, you must remember! I lost my new watch and you found it behind the seat!"* His son's eyes had sought his. The disbelief that his father had no clear memory of what had been such an important event for him, rapidly turned to frustration. *"Oh Dad! Mum, you tell him what happened, perhaps then he'll remember!"* He recalled how his wife had said, rather cuttingly, 'it seemed that lately he had been rarely aware of who he was with, let alone where he was.'

·

"The reality," continued the voice, "of the past being history, tomorrow being a mystery and today being a gift, which is why it is called the present, is ignored by most people. When your ego sees security in *ends*, rather than *means*, your life, and your happiness, becomes results oriented. The cry of: 'I just want to be happy' comes from attaching yourself to those results as they are seen as the key to that happiness. They are not the key, however."

"But surely the end result *is* what is important?" questioned the man. "That's *why* you do what you do."

"Your happiness does not wait at a particular station for you, it is already on the very track of your life. When you live in the here and now, and *let go* of whatever the result will be, your full energy can focus on the process of your life. You dissipate your power when you attach yourself to the result because you do not have any control over it. You only have control over the process."

The man was having difficulty in accepting this idea. It conflicted with what he had always thought.

"How can that be?" he asked. "Surely you have to keep the result in mind and surely you have to have some control over it?"

"Keeping in mind the result you expect to achieve is not the same as attaching yourself to it," answered the voice. "The burden you give to yourself of continually seeking happiness comes from wanting to control or manipulate results. When you project yourself into how the future *must* come out for you you're upsetting the process of allowing things to take their course. Holding on to something causes you to want to force the issue and that very action of pushing harder can drive what you want further away."

The man considered the time when he had desperately wanted a girlfriend and yet the harder he had tried, the less success he seemed to have had. Eventually he had stopped forcing his attention on them and trying to get them to notice him. Amazingly enough, he had started a relationship soon after, one that was just what he had been hoping for. He winced to himself, remembering how he had then forced the speed of the relationship and lost her.

"Everything in nature, of which you are a part, follows a process", continued the voice. "When you try to impress someone you end up with the opposite effect. Consider nature. You do not see a tree trying to grow faster than it can. You do not see a river taking the shortest route to the sea. It takes the path of least resistance yet it always gets where it wants to go and has no attachment to the result. If you can accept that the universe is in balance and everything is in its right place, at the right time, you become able to let go of results.

"Of course at the same time you keep your objective in mind. Otherwise you risk overlooking the numerous meaningful coincidences that arise to help you in your life. When you do not live in the here and now how can you see those opportunities?"

"What do you mean by *meaningful coincidences*?" the man asked in a surprised tone.

"They are occasions which deliver opportunity to you, although they are often obscure and seemingly absurd at the time. Brought about by a powerful energy, transmitted by your most dominant thoughts, these coincidences are meaningful to whatever your current objective may be. You literally attract those people and situations which are in concert with your dominant thoughts."

"Well I was not aware of any meaningful coincidences that brought me any opportunities", interjected the man.

"This is a universal law of like attracts like and, because it is immutable, it will continue to work whether you are aware of it or not. Even if you had not chosen to consider what they could mean, when these serendipitous events were actually coinciding, you had still brought them about."

The man searched his memories for unusual events that he had chosen to ignore. Things he had just not considered as relevant at the time and dismissed as being, well, just a coincidence. The occurrences that came most prominently to his mind were the ones that only seemed to happen when he had hoped something would *not* happen.

*

*"What's the matter?"* asked his wife, while watching him open his post.

*"Nothing"*.

*"Well, your face looks like it's something..."*

It was. A letter from the bank about the overdraft. Everything inside him had told him to contact them, before they contacted him, and he had left it. Just another occasion when he had allowed someone to steal his advantage by phoning or writing to him first.

•

*"Well, hello, what a coincidence..."* the times he seemed to bump into people that he did not want to see! Having to start the conversation with how he had been thinking about them, and how *lucky* it was that they had met right now. He could see how they were fortuitous opportunities for them, but the advantage did not often lay in his favour.

Yet, he did remember times when it had seemed to work well. It had been uncanny the way he had kept bumping into his future wife.

•

*"Hello"*, sitting next to her during a charity concert

arranged by a mutual friend.

"Hello again", filling up with petrol at the garage.

In the bank, "How funny, I never usually use this branch."

It had happened so often that they had even joked, that they must be meant for each other! Mind you she had been in his thoughts almost incessantly. In fact he had hardly been able to concentrate on anything else.

•

"Depending on your thoughts," the voice continued, "the law will work for, or against you, which is why it is important to keep your thoughts on what you want and not on what you don't want. Most people unwittingly concentrate on the latter, which is to their detriment as they literally attract towards them what they don't want."

"Can thoughts be that powerful?"

"They are the seed behind every creation. Nothing exists without thought."

"So if anybody goes through life not knowing what they want, then what they end up with is uncertainty, as I did".

"Yes, except they become certain about what they

don't want. For example when a person has been conditioned to be critical they are able to spot the flaw in an argument, a suggestion, another person, or a career, almost immediately. Their thinking is attuned to what they disagree with, rather than what they agree with. All good points are overlooked in their search. The baby is literally thrown out with the bath water as prejudiced thinking seeks to pigeon hole, label or put in its place whatever is being discussed."

"But isn't it important to look for weaknesses otherwise you cannot be sure whether something will work or not?"

"Yes, if your evaluations are considered together with strengths. There is no balance, however, when judgements are based on opinions which fit a pattern of thinking which is not sure of itself. Think for a moment. When you consider your successes, or failures, which come to your mind the quickest?"

"My failures", the man quietly replied, after a brief pause.

"And when you think of your habits, which come to mind first? Developing your good ones or controlling your bad ones?"

The man thought how intolerant, impatient and argumentative he had been. "Stopping my bad habits", he replied.

"So," the voice said, "when the emphasis of your thought is on bad points over good points, your motivation in life will be distorted accordingly."

"So all the difficulties in my life were directly as a result of my thinking?"

"As your thoughts determine your feelings, your actions and your habits, they affected everything you experienced."

"All my relationships, my situations, my prosperity?"

"Everything."

The man was silent.

Going into business on his own had been more an act of desperation at first. He had always liked the idea of working for himself but, if he was honest, he had lacked the courage. It was strange the way adversity seemed to force you to do things which you would never even entertain at one time.

He had viewed his security as working for a company. In that way you didn't have to worry about being paid, although with his commitments it had never lasted the month it was meant to. He always tried to budget but could never quite get it right. There was always something else that he had to buy, either for himself, or one of his family.

They were a main part of the reason why he had made the decision to work on his own. After his second redundancy he had to do something. He was not comfortable being on 'assistance', although he had convinced himself that the government owed it to him. After all, everyone had agreed that jobs were scarce because of their policies.

That person who had suggested that he take advantage of the situation into which redundancy had thrust him, had been right. He had not recognised it as valuable advice at the time. Well, in time, he had done just that, and, in fact had been too excited to even worry about how he was doing. There were occasions, however, when he had been overwhelmed with doubts. His wife had been supportive and had continued to encourage him, despite the fact that he took his irritation and worry out on her.

She had always advised him to concentrate on what he was good at. Yet, as the business started to grow, it seemed to him that he spent most of his time on things he did not enjoy. Although he believed that his business had filled a gap in the market-place he had been concerned about being a solo player. He remembered feeling relieved when he learned that there were others involved in what he was doing.

Later, though, his relief began to turn to alarm as he began to think how he might be outdone. He would have to find out what others were doing in order to be more competitive. In doing so he now thought about viewing his success in comparison with others and what they were achieving, rather than what he was actually achieving. He became more obsessed with the importance of the next deal, as he saw it as the key, just to stay in business. It became the focus of his new found security.

He remembered now that there was a time when he saw getting married to his wife as his main security. He had told her that he couldn't live without her and she had liked to recall how he had swept her off her feet with his romantic persistence. Their promises of lots of time for each other got harder to keep. He was sure that she had changed after the children had been born.

He certainly had. It was the first time he had felt really responsible towards something. Usually he was so proud of them, but, at times, when under pressure, he would almost mentally view them as a burden. These thoughts sometimes made him feel guilty. Particularly when he couldn't help thinking that they had impeded him from achieving so much more.

Now, despite how hard he worked, his commitments continued to go up and up. More money needed to be put into the business to be able to cope with the new orders he was anticipating. He knew that he had promised his family a good holiday but he would have to tell them that it was just not feasible. They would understand, they would have to, but, if he could only get paid what he knew the service was really worth, then there wouldn't be any difficulty. Yet he dared not risk asking in case he was refused the order, then where would they all be?

*

*"But you promised the children a family holiday. That you'd take us abroad to somewhere hot this year."* His wife was genuinely upset and could not hide her feelings whether she had wanted to or not. *"None of us would mind if it were another camping holiday. What's important is that we spend some time together as a family."*

*"I understand that"*, the man replied. *"But what you don't understand is that I can't even afford to take the time off, let alone the money. We have to get this order, it's the biggest one that we've ever had and I have to be the one to make sure everything runs smoothly."*

*"You say that every time. You never take time off. Order after order after order, that's all you ever think about. What about your family? Aren't we more important than your precious orders?"*

*"It's because you're all so important to me that I'm doing what I have to do. Don't you think I would like a holiday? Of course I would, I want to be able to relax and not keep working. But this one will give us the buffer we have*

*needed. When it comes off we can clear the overdraft and enjoy a great holiday—anywhere you want."*

*"I don't want anywhere. I just want us all to have some time together, the children will be grown up before you know it. Well, you can tell them yourself this time."*

He knew that he had caused hurt, but at the time he had genuinely believed that his actions were in the best interests of his family. Later he realised that they had only deepened the rift that was beginning to exist between them.

He knew also that his wife was really concerned about how he continually pushed himself. She had eventually persuaded him to take a short break, as soon as this particular deal had been concluded. But the compromise had not really eased the tension that was building up in his family.

●

"How could my thinking have been solely responsible for all the difficulties that built up in my life?" the man asked. "Other people were always involved and I was doing the best that I could to provide a home for my family and a service for my business."

"The state of your outer world was merely a reflection

of your inner world", the voice began to answer. "The level of your thinking and the degree of your concentration were directly responsible."

"But what about other people's levels of thinking. Don't they have to carry at least some of the responsibility?"

"No, because they were not responsible for the situations that you had allowed to manifest for you. Your question is, however, an example of the level of thinking that you chose to live by. When you relinquish part of the responsibility to others, for how your life is, you allow them to have control over you, either psychologically, emotionally or physically.

"Imagine two people. One is a person that you want or need something from, be it money, love, attention, an object, or anything at all. The other is someone that you do not want, or need anything from. Ask yourself, was your thinking different in each case?"

The man thought again of the deal that was so important to him. "I suppose I did think differently."

"Why?" the voice asked.

"Because it was important. I was worried about the future."

"Now imagine that there is someone who wants something from you. Are you aware of their thinking?"

The man thought of those people who had almost been desperate to do business with him. Sometimes it was so obvious that he had almost been rude. In fact, at times, he had been. Even when he had done business with them it had never been as relaxed as some of his more confident alliances. "Yes," he answered, "I was aware, for the most of the time at least."

"Did it make a difference in how you treated them?"

The man had to admit that he had always felt in control of them and often would see how far he could push them.

"Yes", he said, in a way that sounded as if he knew what the voice would say next.

"So", the voice breathed out. "You were aware when other people wanted something from you. You felt in control and were able to treat the individual either magnanimously, kindly, patiently, patronisingly, rudely, cruelly, dismissively, understandingly, or whatever. But, regardless of this, you continually put yourself into similar submissive situations whenever someone had something you wanted." The voice paused before continuing.

"There should be no difference in your thinking whether you want something from another person or not. Isn't the key to work at being relaxed when you are with

79

others, as you are when by yourself?"

"Yes, but surely that's easier said than done? You make it sound so simple but how could I have done that?"

"Through concentration, which is the key to all aspects of life. The more you concentrate on what you are doing, the more you begin to live in the present. Whenever you lack concentration you are easily distracted from living in the present. Your mistakes and failures haunt you and your mind is filled with fears of the future.

"It does take hard work and practice but the more you develop the ability to concentrate, the more you begin to see yourself in a more valuable light. When you increase your levels of concentration you rechannel your nervous energy, which you may have previously wasted on anxiety, worry, frustration and despair. These emotions can only disappear by applying your mind to address the cause, be it tangible or intangible, real or imagined.

"Too often, however, people make them temporarily disappear by involving themselves in something entirely different, but they never completely go away. They continue to gnaw away at you until they are forced to manifest themselves in some physical ailment. It is the source that has to be addressed and that source is your thinking."

The man felt a twinge of guilt as he remembered his habit of getting involved in something *new* while hoping a particular *old* problem would go away. "But I always found it hard to concentrate. Even at school all my reports said that I lacked concentration."

"But you were easily able to concentrate on play at that time. The hours just disappeared when you were absorbed in what you enjoyed, didn't they?"

"Yes they did, but again, surely that's different?"

"Different circumstances, perhaps, but it illustrated that you did *have* the ability to concentrate. When properly channelled and focused there is no stronger force available to you than concentrated thought. Nature, however, will take away what you don't use on a regular basis. Your concentration power will wane very quickly if you do not use it as it is intended.

"Your concentration is your direct conduit to listening to your intuition. This guiding wisdom that flows from the source of your inner world can be heard more frequently and more clearly when you are able to concentrate with relaxed intensity."

"But how is it possible to be relaxed and intense at the same time?"

"The power of concentration, in the context of your

mind, means the ability to meditate, or contemplate in order to know. The mind must be in a state of calmness, which means you have to able to relax, and the energy to do this must be intense, in order to be focused. When you *know*, then your outer world corresponds accordingly."

"Know...?" The man paused, "... know what?"

"Know why you are exactly where you are in the world, why you are doing what you are doing at any exact moment, why you are with the particular person you are with, and, who you are."

"It's possible to know *all* that?" The man's voice was incredulous.

"It is possible to know whatever you ask, more importantly, it is possible to understand. Whatever you ask you will receive. People, however, do not know or understand *how* to ask. Most of their lives they spend neither asking nor asking correctly. Because of misguided thinking, including imagining that they do not generally deserve things, they assume an outcome which will match their thoughts.

"Their belief in their self-worth develops self-imposed limitations and their world restricts accordingly. They become afraid to ask for what they want because they do not believe they will get it. The truth is that they neither believe they are worth it, nor yet deserve it."

"I was afraid I would not get an important order if I held out for what I really wanted", the man said, remembering once more how he had dared not risk even asking.

"Every one of your thoughts, has a vibrational energy. Each thought has a particular frequency and all signals you emit are picked up subliminally by others. The degree that you believe you will *not* receive, what you ask, is in proportion to the vibration you send out. As your mind is constantly attracting vibrations that harmonise with it, whatever you believe will create your reality. Everyone is what they are, because of the dominating thoughts which occupy their minds. You can be in command of every situation of your life when you can control your thinking. When you control your thinking, you can determine the feelings that make you act the way you do.

"Using the direct conduit of concentration, in order to listen to your intuition, your spirit's guiding voice, however, is not possible when you are not in command of your thoughts. It follows that if you are unable to listen to your intuition then your spirit has an even harder task in its quest."

The man listened intently, the voice was taking another of his simple questions and turning it into something fine and purposeful. It made him feel he had mattered, and, maybe, he was made to do something more.

"Your spirit seeks to experience personal fulfilment in order that the highest levels of consciousness can be attained. In this way it follows a path of constant growth. Its dilemma is that although it can receive the flow of wisdom, from an Infinite Source to guide its path, it is blocked by your mind's self-limiting beliefs from expressing it outwardly.

"All the spirit can do is allow the feeling of torment inside you to grow until you attract a big enough adversity that knocks you from your current course. To, literally, force you to change your thinking. If it happens that you alter course, and change your thinking, then you begin to grow spiritually. If, however, as too often happens, you choose to take the same route at life's cross-roads, that the dark nights of the soul lead you to, then you arrive in the same situations that you were experiencing before."

"I see now why you said earlier that everything in my life was affected by my thinking, or rather lack of it, as I refused to ever listen to myself." The man felt light-headed. What he had refused to understand, before now, appeared so simple. He became aware of all the times he had ignored his intuition, almost 'on purpose'.

Like the occasions when everything inside had warned him about saying something that he might regret;

when he had spoken the words, in spite of the inner message telling him that they would deeply offend. As soon as the words had left his lips he regretted them, but, he had always managed to rationalise, to himself, that the other person 'had had it coming'. They had been asking for it and deserved it. Perhaps they *had*, he began to think. Perhaps they had, in turn, because of *their* thinking! If that were the case, then surely their thinking would affect his actions towards them.

"If everyone is individually sending out vibrations," he asked, "how can anyone be certain that they are controlling their own actions? It may be that I never asked for what I wanted because I received their signal not to." As he asked the question he wondered if perhaps he had not fully understood what was being explained after all.

"When you are conscious of listening to your intuitive guide you know that you are in control. You become your own influence. But I will explain further.

"Ripples of water flow out from the point where a stone breaks its surface. Larger ripples from a larger stone, thrown at another point, will always wash over the smaller or weaker ripples. It is the same with the metaphysical vibrations that all individuals send out.

"Positive thoughts have a stronger wavelength than negative thoughts, which have a weaker configuration. All the thoughts, that you send out, couple with similar frequencies. So you always draw the situations, conditions, people and circumstances that are in tune with the same frequencies.

"The resulting actions of your thoughts do influence others in their perception of you, but any treatment of you is dominated by their own level of thinking. Remember though, like-minded individuals attract each other, so, although each is unconsciously creating situations which may be shared by others, each is also perceiving them differently. Regardless of whether your thoughts are positive or negative you will manifest the situations conducive to creating the actual reality of your thought.

"Now," the voice continued, "there are four levels of vibration in the physical plane. In their ascending order they are the physical, emotional, mental and the intuitive. The key to success is to use them all in together, which is what was intended. To do this they must operate in the correct sequence, which is that the higher levels control the lower levels. Unless you seek to *consciously* be aware of yourself, you *un*consciously operate from that level which your dominant thoughts occupy.

"For example, when your thought energy in life is concentrated on the physical and emotional levels, your concern is with having enough food, drink, and sleep; and with having enough material possessions and wealth. You are preoccupied with emotional needs, desiring gratification, and wanting to have power and control over others."

The man recognised that he had mainly operated in the first two levels. The physical, because when he was unwell, he had allowed it to dominate his day. And the emotional, since he could not concentrate whenever he had become upset. As for his intuitive level, it had never been recognisable to him.

"As each ascending level, however, has direction over the one below it, a far stronger thought frequency is emitted. When you activate the intuitive level you automatically cause your mental level to think positively, your emotional level to be good and your physical body to act correctly. In utilising your intuition all four levels begin to work in harmony, from the inside out."

The man reflected that there had certainly not been harmony in his life. Perhaps there had been occasions when he had felt intuitive insights, but he had always ignored them.

"The vibrational strength that your thoughts send out increase dramatically. Instead of wanting to control others all the time, you begin to appreciate them. Although you indeed have the power at this level to control others, there is not the need or desire to. Moreover the selfish desire to exploit others on a 'what's in it for me?' basis is now a desire to seek ways to co-operate with others.

"As your thoughts turn their attention from your personal self they begin to focus on your universal self. The more you understand the Universe the more you acknowledge that everything that exists is a vibration and, as such, you enter into a realisation that you are not separate from it, but are part of it all. With this acknowledgement comes an understanding of how you will receive by asking."

The man wanted to admit that, but he had never liked to ask, because when he did, he always expected there to be some conditions attached. He also had to admit to himself that even when he had asked in his mind for something, he had strong doubts about ever receiving anything. While reflecting on what he had just listened to, however, he found it hard to accept that there was so much to understand before one could learn how to ask correctly.

"But throughout my life", he began to ask, "there was certainly no-one who was able to share with me what you have. How is it possible to know these things?"

"The wisdom and understanding which transcends all knowledge learned by tuition can be acquired by learning to deeply listen to yourself. This is all that is necessary in order for you to know all that you are and all you should do."

"If that is the case, and it is there for our benefit, for the benefit of everyone, why is there not a simple way to access it?"

"There is," replied the voice calmly, "and it is the only true key to success."

The man heard the anticipation in his words as he asked: "What is it?"

"Faith. Plain and simple faith."

"The trouble with you is that you just don't believe in yourself enough! Have a bit more faith in what you're doing."

"I do have!" He said, but in truth he was only saying it for the sake of defending himself. She was right though. He was losing faith in what he was doing, fast, and beginning to feel quite scared. His business was just not going as planned and he had been seeking reassurance for what he was doing from his wife.

"Well you certainly don't seem to show it!"

Watching her now, he could see that she was exasperated with him because of the worry that he was putting on her shoulders. She was so occupied with looking after him and the young children that perhaps he should not have burdened her with his business worries. It only made her feel insecure.

"Of course I do, I have to in my business. I'm only telling you because I need to tell someone."

Looking at himself, lying, stretched out on the sofa, he was surprised at how much he had put on weight. When he was worried he had always seemed to eat and drink more. Certainly he drank more than he should.

*"If I notice, then why shouldn't others notice. Some of your 'business colleagues' certainly seem to know you better than I do. They should do; you're always lunching with them."*

What was she implying? Surely she hadn't suspected anything about Her so soon. He had been too careful for that. No, it's nothing.

*"You know that taking people to lunch is an important part of my business. It's the best way to build up contacts and to build people's confidence in you."*

Yes, he thought, it had been best to just ignore it and carry on.

*"Yes, and very expensive. I never get taken out to lunch anymore. I'm just told that we can't afford it! Perhaps if you didn't spend so much on impressing people, you would have a bit more money for us. I've already told you that the children need new school clothes."*

Not this again. The times he had to explain that business money was different to personal money.

*"I've told you that I have to invest in building*

92

*relationships before I can get anything back."*

*"Oh I'm sure you're getting back what you want!"*

There was another innuendo. He didn't feel comfortable but he could see that he wasn't giving any sign of it away. He could not ignore it this time, otherwise it would be obvious that he was hiding something.

*"What do you mean by that? You know that I'm doing everything I can to improve business."*

She turned to glance at the television which had been quietly on, unaware that it was not commanding its usual attention.

*"Not what, who, and you know who I'm referring to. You're always having lunch with her. I saw her name in your diary."*

Safe, he thought. It had been clever of him to put Her name in the diary. He knew his wife regularly checked where he was. It was something she had always done in case she had to get in touch with him urgently.

*"Then you know that she acts for the company I am relying on for my next big order. If I don't get it, then I really will have a serious situation."*

As he watched himself he was surprised at the coolness of his reply, despite the pangs of conscience. He became aware of the fact that he seemed to view his conscience on the basis of "will I be found out?" rather than "is it right or wrong?"

His saw his wife sigh and make a final response as she got up to leave the room.

*"I know, I know, always the 'big' order. Well I would have thought that the amount of orders you've had in the past should have given you all the faith in yourself that you needed."*

•

It was true, the man now reflected, certainly a lot of business had been done in the past. But, if he was honest, he had begun to rest on his laurels and in an arrogant way at that. Perhaps, in truth, his arrogance had increased to hide his lack of confidence.

He certainly felt insecure if he did not receive the orders he wanted, and took it personally when people said no to him. His faith in himself had indeed taken a knock and if what he had learned at those seminars, that he had attended, were anything to go by, so had his self-esteem. Yet he felt good when he had been around Her. There had been something about Her that had him, literally, spellbound.

Admittedly he had encouraged Her attention but he

was sure that she had felt the same way also. He had been unaware, at the time, that he was becoming obsessed and continually arranged all his work movements around Her. Anyway having a relationship with Her actually seemed to restore his faith in himself. She just wouldn't be interested in anybody, they had to be special. Yes, he thought she had made him feel special, or was it a feeling of pride?

•

"Faith forms the substance of all your expectations", he heard the voice continue. "Whenever we ask something of ourselves it is necessary to persist until we achieve it, and the degree to how much you persist, is a measure of the belief you have in yourself."

The man thought how persistent he had been in developing his illicit relationship. He had thrown caution to the wind and had been playing with fire. He remembered how badly his emotions had been burned as he asked: "But what if your persistence is not actually in your interest, yet you are blind to it, at the time? Is that still having faith in yourself?"

"Used positively faith becomes a force which holds the promise of all things hoped for, but as yet, unseen, coming to fruition. There can be no absence of faith, however, and, used incorrectly, it carries the premonition of our deepest fears and unseen darkness. There is a constant battle of faith and reason, on one side, and emotion and imagination on the other. The outcomes are optimism and certainty, or cynicism and despair."

"But isn't faith part of your emotions?" asked the man, wincing as the word 'despair' reminded him how he had felt?

"Do you remember when you learnt to swim?" asked the voice in return.

•

*"I won't let go"*, his father had said. He had been excited about learning how to swim but also nervous.

*"Just... please... don't... whatever you do"*, he heard himself say. It was said for assurance more than anything else. He had reasoned out, perfectly well, in his young mind, that an unsupported body would not necessarily sink. After all, he had seen lots of people swimming and floating in the water. It was almost as if his reasoning had helped him to have faith in being able to do so, also, but then he remembered his father letting him go. He had suddenly

ceased to believe anything of the sort as his imagination and emotions made him get into a panic about going under.

*

"My senses and emotions seemed to destroy the faith in what I really knew to be true", he answered the voice.

"When you allow just your emotions to have control over your faith, then you will tend to call on its force, only, whenever it suits you. True faith is to have the belief to carry on doing something, or to continue to work towards something you truly believe in, and to keep on until you win through, and beyond, *even though* the feeling you had, when you started out, has long since left you or been replaced with another."

"What about doubts though? Doesn't everyone have nagging doubts about what they are able to do, or ask for?"

"Reasoned, or intuitive, doubts are healthy. Indeed it is not until you question your faith, for example, that you are able to grow spiritually. But gnawing self-doubt is emotionally based and emanates from the conditioned you, never the true you.

"Faith exists in everyone and its growth is in direct proportion to the degree that you are true to yourself. As it grows its power enables you do anything that you set your heart on. To ask your intuition in faith means to expect to receive an answer. It does not mean to give up asking after a short period of trying because it has not appeared to work in the time you allotted to give it a try.

"Every person who has ever lived," continued the voice, "has asked themselves the same questions of 'Who am I?' and 'Why am I here?' Amazingly, far too few have persisted enough to receive an answer. Both their reasoning and intuition tell them that there is an answer to be had, but their emotions are allowed to win through, by allowing the urgency of living take the place of life's importance. The growing ego prefers to develop itself with that Pride which is the most damaging of all vices. It is this feeling of Pride that directly distorts all the wonderfully inherent, made-for-life qualities that are so important."

The man felt concern when he heard the words, feeling of Pride. Wasn't that the feeling that he had remembered earlier? "But isn't feeling pride in something good?"

"The kind I am referring to is the Pride that leads to all other vices", replied the voice. "The self-conceited one, rather than a wholesome self-respect. There is no fault which makes a person more unpopular, and no fault of which everyone is more unconscious in themselves. Yet the more Pride one has, the more one dislikes it in others."

"How, then, does anyone know if they are being proud?"

"The easiest way is to ask yourself, 'How much do I like it when other people reject me, refuse to take notice of me, patronise me, or show off?'"

"I used to get really annoyed at anyone who was the centre of attraction at a party", the man said. "Is that because I really wanted it to be me?"

"Each person's Pride is in competition with everyone else's Pride. If someone is doing something better than you, then you consider them to be your rival."

That was exactly how the man had felt. "Is it Pride, then, that makes people keep demanding more and more?"

"Being competitive, by nature, Pride has been the chief cause of misery in nations, as well as every family. Pride gets no pleasure out of having something, only out of having more of it than the next person. People are not proud because they are rich, clever or good looking. They are proud of being richer, cleverer and better looking than others. In the impossible event of everyone being equally rich, clever and good looking, what would there be to be proud about. It is the *comparison* that makes you proud, the pleasure of being above the rest and feeling *special.*

"Once the element of competition has gone, Pride has gone. Understanding this is important, as Pride is a spiritual cancer. As your Pride makes you feel more special than others, however, you *unwittingly attract* the fall that your continuing actions make inevitable. Your spirit, fighting to remove this cancer, welcomes this event. It knows that it is not possible to use the power of faith while Pride eats up your humility, common sense and contentment. For only in humility will your faith assist you to know yourself, and, in turn, you will then receive whatever you ask."

The voice paused. "Tell me about your fall."

*"Good to see you again, sir; we have your usual table ready for you."*

He liked that. It was great to be treated with respect. Mind you he deserved it, after all he had brought enough business to the place. But that wasn't the only reason. He was important. He was 'somebody' in town and he should be treated as such.

It hadn't always been like this though. There were times when he had been treated disdainfully, even dismissively. Not just by this place, either. To him, it felt like he had experienced that at most places, when his business had not been going too well. He had been determined to change things and he had. Once he had managed to get those orders under his belt everything had gone better. People had started to seek him out for business now, and so they should.

*"Oh, by the way sir, your colleague telephoned to say that he would be about ten minutes late. Would you prefer to wait at your table, or take a drink at the bar?"*

'I would *prefer* that he was waiting for me', the man thought. Late. Who does he think he is? After suggesting we have lunch together, he was lucky I was able to fit it in. Late! I doubt if he would even get into this place if I hadn't offered to make the reservation.

*"I'll go straight to the table... Thank you."* He put emphasis on the word 'go', dismissed the word 'wait', and smiled to himself. He was certain that because he would be sitting at the table first, his client would feel even more embarrassed about keeping him waiting.

He liked this table. It was the one he had specifically wanted for some time and he had eventually got it, although it had cost him a small fortune in tips. He considered it worth it, however, as it was like sitting at the head of the table and he could easily survey everyone else.

•

*"Hello there."* He had seen him arrive a moment before and had used the opportunity to glance at his watch as he arrived. 'Fourteen minutes!' He thought.

*"How are you? It's good to see you."*

He knew that his glance had been noted.

*"Sorry I'm late,"* he apologised as he sat down, *"I couldn't find anywhere to park. These places never seem to make enough provision do they? Did you get my message all right?"*

*"Yes, I did, thanks. That's fine. I've only been here a few moments myself."* 'What did he mean *these* places?' he had thought.

*"Still it looks pretty good here. I haven't been here before. Let's hope the food is as good as they make out."*

*"Oh, I can assure you it is."*

Lunch had not been a memorable event. Not because of the food, that, indeed, had been the highlight. It was the business being offered. 'What does he take me for?' He had thought this was going to be an attractive proposition, but this would not be much use to him at all. There was not enough in it for him.

He could see why this person wanted to do business with him, of course. So that he could be introduced to all the valuable contacts that it had taken him years to build. No way. This may be the third one, like this, in a row, but he believed that, with his reputation, he could afford to be dismissive. He remembered being surprised at the time though, almost disconcerted, at the way this person had not seemed to mind whether he got the business or not. If he had been him, he would have certainly felt bothered.

•

Observing the situation, now, the man was aware of something different, something that had not occurred to him at the time. This person had appeared to be actually interviewing him and had not seemed impressed with what he was finding. During the lunch the man had thought that the person's attitude was flippant and disrespectful, even arrogant, yet watching, now, he was conscious that this more aptly described himself. Had he really been like that? Had this person actually not wanted *him* to deal with his business?

•

After lunch he had taken a drive out into the country, He wanted time to think. He was aware that it was because his rise had been so meteoric, that he believed a lot of people were envious of him. They were bound to be. After several moves, he had now bought a prestigious property in a much sought-after area. He was well-positioned and his family didn't want for anything. He was sure of that, although he was not at home as much as, perhaps, he ought to be.

But how could he? There was always something to organise at the office, or someone to see. And he had to see, and make time for, Her. God, he must love Her, even after all this time he couldn't stop thinking about Her. He couldn't even bear the thought of not being with Her, of somebody else taking his place, yet, until now he had lacked the courage to leave his family.

It could be different, now, though. Now that he had persuaded the bank to provide him with a bigger overdraft, he felt much more in control. He planned to buy a cottage somewhere, like that one he had looked at years ago. Somewhere in the country, away from prying eyes, so they could be together. In fact, he thought, if he was careful, no-one would have to find out. It wouldn't do for all his business associates to know what was going on. Although he felt sure they would be all jealous, he was concerned about what they might think or say.

What about everything else though? He would have to give up a lot of that and his wife would insist on the house. On the other hand he wouldn't want his children to suffer, too much, so it would be better for her to have the house for the moment. Anyway, even though the kids were getting older, she wouldn't need such a big place, so he could suggest that he find something smaller for them. After all if he could be happy with a smaller cottage, he felt sure they would too.

He had driven back to the office with the idea of making some calls to put his plans into action. He began to think of what they should do together tomorrow. They had arranged to see each other for the whole day and the thought exhilarated him. They would drive out to see the cottage, that he had arranged to show Her. What a surprise it would be.

He certainly didn't feel guilty. The business was doing fine without him being there all the time. He had already marked down in the diary that he was taking another client out to lunch. In this instance he had blocked out the whole day adding that, as this particular one lived in the country, he would need time to drive out there. 'Perfect', he thought, 'and if no-one is any the wiser, then no-one will get hurt'. Yes, being your own boss had real benefits. You could be a law unto yourself.

The man noticed that he had used his conscience more to direct himself, mainly on the grounds of whether anyone found out, rather than if it was right or wrong. It was as if he had trained it to advise him that he could do anything he liked, so long as no-one found out. Mind you, he remembered, he had not liked the way his conscience sometimes pricked him. He hated the idea of hurting anybody, but he wondered, now, why he had been more concerned about what others thought, rather than what he, himself, thought.

It was quite obvious to him that his belief had been, so long as others didn't find out, or get hurt, that everything and everyone would be all right. The feelings he now had, in watching himself, contradicted this. He did not feel comfortable about the way he had chosen to live.

A lot of people were going to be hurt by his actions, but now he had the realisation, that the most hurt he had been doing, had been to himself. It had been continuous. How had he been able to deceive himself so well, and for so long?

He remembered thinking that he must telephone about the keys for the cottage, as he was returning to the office, when he saw Her car. As always, whenever he saw Her, his heart jumped with excitement. What a coincidence, he thought, he would be able to see Her for real now, instead of just thinking of Her.

His moment of pleasure, however, turned to pain as he

saw that she wasn't driving. She was the passenger and a man, whom he didn't recognise, was at the wheel. He tried to calm his thoughts as he debated following Her, after they had driven past him. Surely she had noticed him? And if not, why not? She had been too involved in conversation, that's why. Mind you, on the other hand, they had agreed not to give away too much in public, but a simple wave couldn't hurt. He was sure that they had both been laughing though. They certainly looked to be enjoying themselves. What the hell was going on?

He kept asking himself stupid, pointless questions. He tried telling himself that it was nothing, but he could not stop the continual doubt from filling his mind.

The man watched himself as he rudely snapped at the people in his office. It wasn't a big office and whatever mood he was in would always permeate throughout.

*"You've had three calls for you while you were out. One from the bank, one from your wife, both to call back, please, and one was to cancel lunch..."*

*"Tomorrow?"* he interrupted while trying not to sound as if he was in a panic.

His secretary was calm, but her eyes had showed a hint of interest in his reaction. *"No, please let me finish, I was about to say, today. Your lunch appointment 'phoned to ask if he could cancel but, after I had said that you had already left, he said not to worry that he would see you anyway. He did say something about being late though, but, that he would 'phone the restaurant and tell them to give you a message."*

The man suspected that his secretary had enjoyed what she had just put him through, but then decided that he was probably being over-sensitive. He was sure she hadn't any knowledge of his life outside the office, yet he became aware of the fact that deceit was exhausting. Lately, he had begun to imagine the worst in every message he received. It was even worse at home. It had got to the point that he jumped every time the 'phone rang, in case it was Her, or someone, who, in all innocence, may say something out of place and he would be caught out.

What was it his wife wanted anyway? It was unlike her to 'phone and not leave an actual message. Usually it was to ask or remind him to get something on the way home. And what about the bank, why should they 'phone?

The man watched himself, fully aware that his imagination had been running riot because it was running in conjunction with his apprehension. Apprehension about what he had just witnessed. What could it mean? He was unable to concentrate, let alone think straight.

*"Make me a cup of tea please"*, he heard himself say. *"whilst I make these calls?"*

Of course, his first call had been to Her to see if She was now back at the office. There was no reply on Her direct line so he next called reception to ask if she was in today. The receptionist was unhelpful so he decided against leaving a message.

His second call was to his bank. The manager was pleasant enough to him but wanted to know whether he wished to instruct a transfer from his business account into his personal account, as the latter had gone way over the limit. Although he had arranged for this type of reminder to be done, he was surprised that it had happened so quickly.

Perhaps he had been spending much more than he had realised. He thanked the manager, asking him to follow the suggested action, adding that they must have some lunch together very soon.

He then started to telephone his wife.

"You cannot be a law unto yourself. There are Universal Laws, independent of you, that make this thinking futile. These Laws control you, and it is your conscience that guides you to follow them."

The man stopped wrestling with the memories of how he had used his conscience, as soon as he heard the voice.

"You can view your conscience, if you like, as your internal compass that always points towards the true north, or correct way, of Life's Principles. This is that dynamic of your spirit which guides your self-development and awareness, the elements vital to your growth.

"If you allow external circumstances to magnetise this compass," continued the voice, "you will distort your conscience's guidance and weaken its power. Your natural conscience, which is a special positive emotion, then lies dormant behind your conditioned conscience. This one, in turn, becomes caught up with all your negative emotions. If you do not use your conscience to its full potential, when it does arise, it always brings uncomfortable feelings, even suffering, for it is very unpleasant to face the truth about yourself."

"But isn't the purpose of conscience to make us feel guilty and uncomfortable."

"No, it is not. It is there to point us towards those Universal Principles that create harmony and quality of life. But as conscience is that part of your consciousness, where you cannot hide anything of your conduct, it makes you feel uncomfortable when you are not following those Principles it seeks to make you aware of. To prevent these unpleasant feelings, however, you, in turn, develop methods to use negative emotions, such as anger, fear, suspicion, self-pity and jealousy, as reasons to create justification for your actions."

The man thought of how often he seemed to have been effected by these emotions and asked: "What kind of methods?"

"Methods which cause you to seek to return the same treatment, *because* it was done to you. Methods that make you look to defend or justify your actions. For example, you may justify that because everyone does something, it's all right, or, if no-one will know about something, is not effected, or cannot get hurt, then what does it matter."

Perhaps that thinking had very much been the basis behind a lot of his actions, the man thought. "But what if someone's actions are done purposely to upset you or make you angry? Isn't that in itself enough reason for any defending action?"

"It is a delusion to believe that your negative emotions are created, or caused, through the faults of others, or because of circumstances. Their causes lie inside of you, not outside of you. They are causes which only exist because you mistakenly believe that they are part of you. You create them like some artificial propaganda with which you have identified. They are not you, however, because you are not your emotions.

"As your habitual ways of thinking seek the aim of avoiding unpleasant feelings and realisations about yourself, you become accustomed to think and do things in a certain way. When you have an unpleasant feeling, which you call 'a pricking of your conscience', you automatically seek to justify yourself in order to not feel uncomfortable. If there is no reason to stop this habitual, artificial thinking you begin to believe your own propaganda about yourself. Your tendency was to further develop an attitude of arrogance in your treatment of others, as it was easier to find fault with everything, except yourself."

"What could I have done to develop the thinking, so that I could have used my conscience correctly?"

"Observed yourself internally. Your most significant world is your inner world. In that world is self-awareness, independent will, creative imagination and conscience. Internal observation leads you to understand how your conscience works and how it can be used to create and develop a balanced life."

"Could you explain to me how it is possible to observe yourself internally?"

"In the same way that you can tell whether drinking water is cool or hot, you can learn to distinguish between those cool, comfortable and those hot, disturbing feelings. Watch how your feelings arise when someone criticises or questions you. Notice how you feel when you receive bad news, or good news. See how you arouse waves of depression or excitement respectively. In this way, you begin to differentiate between your true self and your conditioned, false self. Between truth and artificial thinking."

The man thought how defensive he had been about some of his ideas. "I suppose that by observing myself in this way, I would have led to learn that I, perhaps, held false ideas about myself?"

"Yes," replied the voice, "tension results when you attempt to prove that what is really an illusion is a reality. In life it is important to question all those ideas which you feel you must defend. Why are you defending them? Are you simply defending your false self? The truth needs no defence; no justification. It can be explained but never needs defending. Tension and exhaustion arise when you defend yourself and your imaginary ideas about yourself."

The man recalled how uncomfortable he had felt when others had not accepted him in the way he had hoped for. At times he had defended his actions vigorously, rather than risk their rejection. He had always hated rejection.

Anticipating his thoughts, the voice continued. "It is important to notice the different feelings you get when you experience rejection, rather than acceptance. It is wiser to risk rejection at every opportunity as you learn from rejection, not from acceptance, in the same way that a missile stays on target when its gyro rejects a wrong course. Were you ever aware of the false sense of satisfaction that you harboured as a result of a rejection or insult?"

"I remember that I did not talk to a friend of mine for several years after what I thought, at the time, was a direct insult. I admit that I did hold onto the feeling of pain that the experience had given me, but I was not aware that it gave me any satisfaction. Perhaps, on reflection, the very reason I held on to it was because I derived some satisfaction from it."

"There can be no reason, other than a false satisfaction, not to let something go. There is no virtue in suffering pain, hurt or guilt. True understanding and true conscience grow when you cease to enjoy your sufferings. This follows the Universal Law that you have to let go of something, in order to gain freedom from it, in the same way that you have to lose sight of one shore, before you can begin to see another shore.

"It is not because you believe another has cheated or insulted you that you feel resentment towards them. It is because they have exposed your gullibility. But you will not see this until you let go of the resentment. The ego does not want to let go of the resentment, because it gives it more satisfaction, than having to face the truth that you can remove your gullibility forever, through a willingness to learn from your humiliation.

"The truth that damages your ego, however, is the same truth that frees you and strengthens your character. By recognising the feeling of satisfaction, that you derive from indulging in self-hurt, you are able to let go of it and release the energy it was draining from you. This is important as, like all inner and outer world reflections, the energy with which you indulge your self-hurt is the same energy you use to hurt others.

"Through consistent self-observation and evaluation you could have become more conscious of yourself, more aware. As your self-awareness is the ear to the voice of conscience, you become able to listen, with greater clarity, to the directions your conscience gives you. This leads you to understand those Universal Laws that are so vital in all that you do and in all of your relationships and communications with others in your life.

"These Laws will always have their paradoxical effect whether they are understood or not. The need to dominate or control people to obtain their respect will have the opposite effect. Any action you take to appear strong with others will be read as a weakness. When you give up the mood to appear impressive and important you no longer feel the tension due to your artificial behaviour."

"So many times I behaved in a way that I thought the other person wanted me to behave. Is that why I sometimes felt so exhausted?"

"It is better to behave the way you really are, even if it ends a relationship. It is pointless to suppress yourself in an effort to hold, win or influence another. When you are unreal, so are all of your rewards. It makes no sense to try to change the way others treat you by learning calculated behaviours, or attitude techniques, in order to be in charge. This only creates inner conflict for you.

"What you really want in your relationships is command over yourself, not over them. Looking for approval, expressing contrived concern for well-being, explaining yourself to others, and trying to impress another, are all examples of self-sabotage while you misguidedly think that you are strengthening your position with others. By understanding yourself you begin to understand where others are coming from.

"With self-evaluation you could have established your definite aims in life. You would have then been aware of what was important in your life and been able to establish your values. Meaningful values which your conscience aligned to guiding Principles. Upon this foundation any goals that you desired would have been reached as a matter of course."

"But goals are something that I did have", the man stated defensively. He had learned how to set his goals and objectives at one of the seminars he had attended, when he first started the business. They had certainly made a difference in his approach to planning his life.

"Goals are meaningless if they are not developed in the framework of meaningful values. Unless they are, there is a feeling of empty satisfaction, after they have been achieved", the voice replied.

"Not many of my goals did satisfy me. In fact I suppose many of them were intended to impress, although I thought that I really wanted them, at the time."

The man thought now about the house he had bought. He had wanted it for the wrong reasons. It was not a practical home for a family. His wife had certainly not felt comfortable about it, it was too big, too lonely.

He too, if he was honest, had never felt it was home. But it had looked so impressive, and it was positioned so well, that people could not help but notice it, even from afar. So what if it had stretched his finances a bit. It had been in line with his goal to be somebody important in the town and, in that respect, it could not be better.

He was now painfully aware that if he had established his values first, then he would not have even considered it as a goal. Values. His had been so shallow, so changeable, and were to cause him unbelievable pain and regret.

*"Didn't you get the message that it was urgent?"* It was unusual to hear stress in his wife's voice. She was always so calm.

*"What's the matter?"* There was no point in saying that he had 'phoned as soon as he got the message because he hadn't.

*"Your sister 'phoned. It's your father. He's taken a turn for the worst and the hospice has advised that we go up within the next forty-eight hours."*

It was not unexpected. His father had cancer and had recently gone into a hospice for the care and attention that he needed.

*"How is he?"* He heard himself ask, although he already knew the answer.

*"Not well,"* his wife said quietly, *"he's sleeping most of the time but he knows that we'll be there in the morning. I've already telephoned and asked the hospice to give him the*

*message. I thought you would want to leave tonight. We can
stop for something to eat on the way."*

His first thought was Her. What about his plans?
Tomorrow was important to him. Surely they could go up
tomorrow evening. His conscience pricked him once more as
he said: *"Tonight and away tomorrow. Couldn't we leave
tomorrow evening? I have a pretty full day tomorrow."*

*"You're not being serious are you?"* His wife paused
before continuing. *"How can you even think that? The next
day after tomorrow might be too late. I thought you might
want to see him tonight but we could not get a hold of you in
time. Anyway...",* she paused once more, *"I asked your
secretary to check your diary before I made any arrangements
and she said you only have one 'lunch' appointment out of
town. I suggest you come home right away, we'll have to
leave soon."*

He thought she was going to put the 'phone down on
him at that point so he quickly added: *"Yes of course we
must go immediately. I was only thinking out loud and just
couldn't think straight for a moment. Thanks for organising
everything. See you in half an hour."*

\*

Watching himself drive home the man reflected on how he had reacted. He had been continually controlled by his emotions. He felt surprise and a little contempt for this somewhat overweight, flustered individual who was driving too fast. He had not been aware, before, that many of his actions had been not only self-centred but also irresponsible. They had certainly not been principle-centred.

He also remembered the earlier words he had heard, that frustration came from trying to control a result. Even though the circumstances were perhaps inappropriate he could now plainly see that it was only possible to have control over the process of what you were doing. His mind had been almost continually in the future, always holding on to the result, which, to him, had been the most important thing.

Now, regarding himself in retrospect he saw that despite all his plans for the next day, a different outcome would happen. He could see how, in truth, he had wasted so much of this present life, the here and now, as he had heard, anticipating future outcomes.

Even when he was with Her he would talk about what it would be like in the future. Even when he was kissing Her, rather than living in the moment, his mind was on where it was all leading to. When he was at home his mind was with

Her, and, when he was with Her, his mind was on when he would have to leave to go home! The realities were ludicrous! He had been literally wasting precious moments which would never be replaced!

He was shocked at the realisation of how unaware he had been. And he thought he had been living his life to the full! He thought he had been pretty clever in those days. Yet if his actions had been different, if he had been conscious of what he had been doing to himself, then perhaps what happened to him, would not have happened.

He now watched as he saw himself park by a telephone box on the way home. He had already tried to contact Her before he had left the office but without success. "Where the hell was She?" he asked himself. He listened to the ringing tone while he wondered what to do if he could not get hold of Her. She would be driving out of town to meet him at their usual rendezvous point and he would not be there. Still no reply.

•

Everyone was quiet for most of the drive. Although the children seemed more pleased about having an unexpected day off school than anything else, they sensed the tense atmosphere emanating from the front of the car, and kept quiet.

*"Did you manage to reorganise your appointment?"* His wife asked.

*"Yes."* He lied. *"No problem at all."* He did not feel like talking much, other than in monosyllables. His emotions continued to be in turmoil.

We really *do* do it to ourselves, he told himself, as he negotiated his way through the traffic. Hell is not a place you go to. You create your own retribution from your actions. And purgatory must be a place you carry around with you that makes you uncomfortable wherever you are.

He turned on the children, who had begun laughing and messing around in the back of the car. *"Will you two shut up, I can't hear myself think!"* He heard his wife sigh at his impatience.

His anger and frustration dissolved into desolation. He felt numb and desperate and for what reason? It wasn't because of his father and it couldn't be because of Her. Although, he was blaming Her. But how could it be Her fault. More than likely she *is* living in the present moment. How would she know that he needed to get hold of Her? He had convinced himself that she spent her time waiting for him to call and he had not liked hearing that she too had a life to lead. After all, as she had been quick enough to remind him during a recent row, *he* was the one who was married.

'Self-hurt', the man decided as he watched himself. 'I'm indulging in self-hurt, wallowing in self-pity. And I'm treating others, my family, in the same way. I'm beating them up mentally.' His thoughts went to his father. He had not seen much of him after his parents had divorced. After living with the woman he had left home for, it had not worked out for him. The woman had soon left him and he had taken a job on the other side of the country shortly afterwards.

He knew that his father had frequently written and called his mother in the hope that they could give it another go together. But nothing ever came of it. Perhaps his mother had been too hurt, but he thought that the main reason was that she had lost respect for his father. *"How can you love someone if you don't respect them anymore?"* she had told him and his sister once.

His father had eventually married again and he remembered the resentment he felt. But why, he thought now? What business had it been of his anyway? It would be like his father interfering in his life, yet, he had even tried to make his father feel guilty. He wondered if his children would hold the same feelings towards him, after all, what he was planning was hardly dissimilar.

He hoped that they would understand. He really loved them. But what was love? He had really loved his wife, once. None so much as when she was actually giving birth to their children. Those were occasions when he was truly conscious of living in the present moment. The togetherness that they had shared in those moments was difficult to describe. If love was only pure when it was unconditional, then he understood that he had felt it. Love like that did seem to have a divinity about it. But why could it not last?

*

*"Penny for them?"* He heard his wife say and watched himself turn to her as he registered the question.

*"Oh, I was just thinking about Dad. It's so sad that it's come to this for him. He always had such plans."*

*"Sounds a bit like you then."* He noticed that her remark was cutting. Revisiting the event now he was certain it had been because she had felt increasingly insecure. His attitude had certainly given her reason to be. Was it that obvious that he had cooled towards her? He wondered if he would have known if she was having an affair.

*"What do you mean by that? My plans have worked for us. We have a nice house and a good business! My father never worked for himself, although he always talked about it. But he was always working. Perhaps if my father had more balance in his life, he would have been happier."*

He noticed his wife looking at him, in amazement.

*"Balance! You're a fine one to talk. The only balance you have ever thought about is your bank balance!"*

The bickering continued for most of the journey until the kids said they were hungry and couldn't they all eat soon. He took the opportunity to call and the 'phone was at last answered.

*"Where've you been? I've lost count how many times I've called you."*

*"I'm sorry."* She replied. *"I didn't want it to be like this..."*

He was talking, rushing to get the words out. *"Listen, I can't be long I just needed to tell you that I can't make it tomorrow. I'm on the way to see my father, he's dying."* He had paused, something was not right. He had wanted to make Her feel guilty about not being available, but she just sounded sad.

*"I'm sorry, ...I wondered why you sounded so upset."*

*"Yes I am, but I'm more upset that I can't see you*

*tomorrow. I had a surprise planned for you."* He impulsively decided to tell Her. *"I was taking you to see a cottage that is perfect for us."*

*"Oh dear, you haven't seen my letter have you?"*

*"What letter?"* Then he knew. *"Oh, too busy being driven around by some infatuated office boy to tell me yourself, face to face eh?"* He couldn't believe he had said it that way, but he found it hard to stop himself. He was in a state and She had put him there.

*"He is not an office boy, he's my new partner. I'm leaving to work with him, and I think it's better if you and I stop seeing each other!"* she replied coolly.

Her tone began to take command of him immediately.

All he could do was say sorry. It could not finish like that. They had to talk. He had to go, or his family would be wondering what was holding him up. His suspicion and jealousy had been rewarded.

*"Who were you telephoning?"* his wife enquired.

He had to lie again, and not very convincingly he felt. Fortunately it was not pursued. Perhaps she was not going to waste her energy in being further upset or perhaps she just didn't want the bickering to start again. She was right about one thing though. His life was certainly not in balance.

138

"Is it ever possible for a perfect state of balance to exist?" the man asked.

"It is the first Principle of the Universe." The voice replied. "Your spirit seeks perfect balance as it knows that it is only through balance that its level of consciousness can grow. It knows that this is possible as it is already an integral part of God's Universe and the whole basis of the Universe is its perfect equilibrium. It has to be for the planets to revolve in harmony without collision."

"But balance, like that, is on a much different scale for mankind isn't it?"

"It is only your perception of balance that makes it so. Nature is God's living example of balance, yet mankind, even though a part of Nature, chooses to ignore that wisdom demands balance. Human beings are the only creatures who do not have balance in their lives, unless they create it by choice.

"Most people are unaware that they need to establish equilibrium, as a principle, in order to develop their true nature. Their perception of balance is a mid-point between opposites. Doing more of something, by doing less of something else, does not necessarily achieve balance."

"But wasn't I achieving balance when I tried to see more of my children by doing less of my work?"

"Inner balance is not established by setting two polar opposites against each other, as miserliness against extravagance, but by combining two necessary qualities together such as bravery with caution. The balance needed with any relationship is not between attention and non-attention. It is to have attention with intention. Children, in particular, will know whether you spend time with them because you want to, or because you ought to.

"Each quality needs to be balanced by its complementary element. The balance needed by faith is understanding; by intuition is reason; by emotion is intellect; by peacefulness is energy; by aspiration is humility; and by zeal is discretion."

"I wish now that I had actually spent more time with them than I did." The man said. "I wish now that I had done many things differently. Thinking about it, I don't believe that any of my aspirations and ambitions were tempered with humility, or, for that matter, patience."

"Having aspirations and being ambitious is important for survival and growth. Your desire to succeed is positive but, preoccupation with personal ambition that keeps you constantly wound up, frustrated and impatient about what your future will bring, is not. Being in balance means having the right motives not just making the right moves."

"I was certainly always looking to make what I thought were the right moves and see the right people. Those were the goals I set myself in order to succeed."

"You will always be eventually recognised for what you are, not what you try to be. Balance is created from establishing your values, knowing what you stand for, and what is important to you. Goals, not based on these priorities, will often lead you away from what you want, although you are not conscious of this, at the time, because the actions to achieve them cause your imbalance."

"But there were times when the only thing that was important to me was peace of mind. That was a good goal wasn't it? Yet the more I sought it the less I seemed to feel it."

"Peace of mind is sought by more people than anything else. But there is always something new over which to seek peace of mind. Your ego urges you to find peace of mind over this relationship, or that possession; over this thought, or that action. But which of your minds are you seeking peace over? Your spiritual higher self or your egotistical conditional self?

"True peace of mind," the voice continued, "can only come from contentment of your spirit. This is derived by expressing itself through you, when moderation of your ego allows this. Nothing outside of you could ever provide it. Relationships and possessions are not responsible for attaining peace of mind, although they are believed to be.

"Only you are responsible for you so your first responsibility is to be responsible. Only in this way can you develop the discipline required for balance in your life. When you are in balance your vibrational energy is raised to a very high level. You literally attract a harmony into your life that effects everything you do and everyone you meet.

"Conversely, the low energy that imbalance emits will attract the adverse conditions of tense relationships, illness and even accidents. Either way, you are responsible. Understand this." The voice paused as though to give emphasis to the words that were to follow. "The key to developing balance, which is vital to your spirit's quest, can only be through acceptance of full personal responsibility."

*

*"I can't believe that you have allowed this to happen!*
*You used the money my mother left me to start your business.*
*And now, because of your stupid irresponsibility, you're*
*telling me you needed to borrow more!"*

Never before had he seen his wife so upset and angry.
*"I was assured that it was a good investment. The return*
*would have provided the extra capital the business needed.*
*It's not my fault!"*

*"Yes and why did you need it. You told me the*
*business had never been so good."*

He thought that it had been. Perhaps he had just
convinced himself it was. He had to admit that since losing
Her everything seemed to be falling to pieces. Most of all
him. Unable to concentrate he had recently lost his biggest
order due to a stupid error, and one which was not his fault
at that.

New business had not transpired as expected and it
had been impossible to meet his commitments which had
been larger than anticipated. Hearing about an investment
which promised a quick return with very minimal risk,
negligible in fact, he saw the opportunity to sort out his cash
flow problem.

It had not worked and desperately he had worried

135

which way to turn. He wanted to rectify the situation before telling his wife, but did not immediately know how. And now it was too late. She had found out. Their personal account had been up to the limit and the bank had written for instructions.

As the man watched himself he was surprised at how helpless he looked. He believed he had always behaved responsibly, yet he began to realise that perhaps he had just been good at shifting it on to others.

•

"If an event is completely beyond your control how is it possible to take full responsibility?" He asked the voice.

"By always accepting responsibility you will be able to focus your energy on creating solutions. In this way you create something positive from a difficult situation and can clearly see the opportunity that lies in adversity. Opportunity always exists in any adversity, but it will remain unseen if your energy is directed on finding fault, or apportioning blame."

"But isn't it important to teach people a lesson for being irresponsible, otherwise how will they learn?"

"You are not responsible for the irresponsibility of

others. What is important is what you are able to learn from the lesson that another's irresponsible action provides you. If someone steals something of value from you, it is your anger and indignancy that causes you to demand recompense and to make that person pay. The shout of 'who's to blame' may cover the culprit's background, society, and government.

"The true lesson," the voice continued, "for you to learn and grow from, is found in the solution, it is not found in the blame. It may be that you need to learn to have less attachment to things. If your attachment to them allows your negative emotions to have such control over you, then it is only by their loss that you may escape the impeding grip that such emotions have over you. Remember you can only gain when you let go."

"But what about the person who stole? Without punishment for the crime, surely, there can be no lesson?"

"Whatever penalty that society deems fit to apply will not teach the culprit a lesson if he or she chooses not to learn from the event. That person may only choose to consider whose fault it was that they were caught. The true lesson may be just one of many for him, or her, to learn personal responsibility."

The man thought about the money that he had lost, and of losing Her. He had blamed both for the reason everything started to go wrong. "But it seems very unfair to have to suffer a lesson if it is somebody else's fault."

"From your spirit's clear perception it is perfectly fair. Only you are able to make yourself suffer. Everything is just the way it is, whether you understand this or not. Every lesson in your life is a blessing, and all your blessings are provided in order that you can choose to grow. Any imbalance will attract situations into your life in order to redress the balance. This is in line with your spirit's quest for personal fulfilment."

Perhaps it was because of its weight that he had repeatedly tried to shift responsibility. The man now admitted this to himself. There had been a couple of occasions in his life, however, when he had experienced the enormous burden personal responsibility carried. Those had been the births of his children.

He remembered an overwhelming sense of joy and a sense of achievement. Yet, on each occasion he held his newly-born children for the first time, these emotions had coupled with a deep sense of responsibility towards them. Their vulnerability fascinated him. They were so fragile, so dependent.

He had promised himself that he would do everything to give them a good life. If pure love could only be unconditional, then he was certain he had experienced that also. But had it lasted unconditionally, he asked himself? In his efforts to fulfil his promises he had often felt insecure in his ability to provide. He had sought reassurance and appreciation from them, almost as a measurement on how well he had performed in his rôle as a father.

It seemed to him, that, at the times when he had been more under pressure than others, they had taken him for granted. But had they? Or had his thoughts on what love was, or wasn't, simply distorted his perceptions? If they really appreciated him then they should be more demonstrative, he had reasoned, didn't they know how lucky they were to have him as a father, they could at least have showed him after all he had done for them.

Yet, why had he always looked for them to be thankful? That would make everything he had done for them conditional. Had he wanted to provide for them in *return* for their love, appreciation and respect or simply *out* of love?

Had he always been so insecure, even about his family? He had *not* made a contract at their birth that he would look after them *only* on the condition that they would love and appreciate him. Yet, here he was remembering how they should have been thankful, after all he had done for them.

He had made them feel guilty for him having to fulfil his own promise to them. Hadn't he similarly been made to feel ungrateful as a child? Although not comprehending what he was supposed to have done as a child, he had taken the *same* action. Unconsciously or not, he had used guilt unfairly. How irresponsible can a parent be? Surely he was the one who should have been grateful for them. They were his family, his anchor and if anyone had taken anything for granted it had been him. And now they were gone.

*

"*What's this?*" His wife had offered to help him at the office since he had to let his secretary go to ease his cash flow.

His heart stopped as he realised she was holding the letter from Her. He had intended to destroy it, but had not been able to. It was as though having the letter allowed him to hang on to his suffering. His mind would not accept that their relationship was over.

From that day onwards things had changed.

*

"*Oh, hi Dad. Mum says not to bother this weekend. She has something else organised. Oh, by the way can you bring the money for the school trip you promised?*"

He had put the phone down slowly after the call. She wouldn't even to speak to him, other than through the solicitors, not even allowing him any opportunity to explain. And he was certain that she was trying to make everything even harder for him. It was obvious to him that she wanted to make him pay, to hold him fully responsible.

At the time he had tried to explain that it wasn't just his fault, and anyway it was all over. She had not been interested, however, in any of the pleadings he had offered in his defence. There was no way she would ever forgive him, she had sworn that. Watching himself now, he could see that he had been responsible for her reaction, but he had been shocked at the speed of it.

Everything was so lonely with no-one to talk to. He had always been so busy when they had all been together. Too busy to even notice them. He had always seemed to have something to do and they got in the way. He hadn't had time for them, yet now, everything was so empty in his life. He needed them now more than ever.

It's true, he thought, as he poured himself another drink, it was I who took them for granted. He found it hard to believe that he had actually planned to leave them. Yet, they had actually left him, ironically because of the same reason he had been going to leave—Her.

It was all so pointless but why did it feel so like that? Perhaps it wasn't what he had really wanted at all, and this was just another case of him being easily distracted by people and situations outside of himself. He had not been in command of himself, as he had so confidently thought. He never had been. How could he have, if all his decisions had been influenced by external factors?

If that was not the case, then why was he so desperate to have his family back, now that they were gone? Would he have felt differently, if the situation had been as he had originally planned, and he was now living with Her? Would living with Her really have given him whatever he had convinced himself he needed?

As the man watched himself pour another drink he began to accept that all of his frustrations in life had come from false desires, and from not getting what he misguidedly thought he had needed. He had never been conscious of what he had really wanted, his true desires.

*

"When you have desires towards another," the voice said, "you persuade yourself that they are able to help or give you what you want. Friction builds up, however, as each person has contrary desires. Your desire, towards another, creates an unconscious insistence that the other *should* or *must* behave the way you wish. When the other person does not, you feel cheated and resentful. You falsely think that your pain has come from the other person's selfishness, when in fact it came from your false desire."

"So my false desires destroyed the relationships that were important to me?" The man asked.

"The reason why many relationships fall apart is because each party tries to receive what the other cannot give. Two people may thrill at the newness and novelty of the other but, when the excitement passes, as it always does, a new direction is sought to fill the feeling of emptiness.

"What is continually sought in another, however," the voice continued, "needs to be first discovered in yourself. For example, it is pointless to call a relationship based on desire by the name of love. It may sound romantic but genuine love is another thing. Only when you are conscious of your true self and have experienced love in yourself, will you recognise it in another."

"So the emptiness and suffering I felt was always caused by what I thought I needed, these false desires?"

"When you do not think beyond your false desires you unconsciously block fulfilment of your true needs. The pain that causes you emptiness is always done to yourself, but it is only because of your emptiness that you become receptive to learn something new. Just as physical pain must be heeded to restore the health of your body, your mental pain can be used as a guide towards spiritual wholeness.

"Freedom from the suffering, that voids in your life bring, is possible. But often the wrong direction is pursued. For example the first impulse, on suffering a loss of any kind, whether of spouse, friend, popularity, comfort, or anything at all, is to escape heartache by chasing after a replacement for whatever you lost."

The man instantly remembered how he had tried to get back with Her when his wife left, without success. "I did that, but why?"

"Because you missed the sense of security, that which you had provided. Having lost the familiar, you seek something else which you hope will become equally familiar. All that happens is that you are left in even deeper despair."

"That's how I felt, but it was all I could think to do."

"It is difficult to stop doing the wrong thing when you mistakenly assume that it is the only thing to do, or your life will fall apart. This thinking is pointless as only the opposite of it is true. When you stop thinking about planning and calculating for a happy and purposeful life your spiritual awareness can begin to grow in its place and you become a unified person."

"What was the other direction I should have taken?"

"The answer is simple, although it may seem difficult, because it goes against all your habitual reactions to loss. You must face your new and unfamiliar situation with a sense of wonder. Observe yourself in what is a new and interesting experience for you. Watch how your state is one of being lost, perplexed, worried and empty with no hope, no expectations and no comfort. Decide to <u>not</u> run away from it and, instead, stay in order to listen to what it can teach you."

The man began to become acutely aware that he had taken the wrong direction. Rather than ever face his own suffering, he had always tried to evade it. He could see now that suffering had to be dissolved, not escaped from.

"When you are able to observe yourself in wonder, you make possible the miracle of your transformation. It is unimportant whether your external conditions change, or not, because this miracle does not occur in your external world. It occurs in your Inner world.

"Your increased awareness allows you to see what facing your suffering can provide. You become aware that the supports upon which you have been leaning, have all been illusory and false. By discarding them, the truth comes to support you completely. Only when you have no support can you be supported."

"That sounds like a riddle. I don't understand the contradiction."

"It is one of the paradoxical truths of your Inner world that is important to understand." The voice began to explain. "If you have a reason for knowing that all is well, for example, because you are financially sound or because you have family and friends, then you have no genuine security."

"Why?"

"Because dependency upon such things breeds fear, for you begin to worry if everything is going so well, how long will it last. You can only know that all is well when you have absolutely no reason for it. In this way you are not relying on any psychological support. Only when you are in this free state can you fully enjoy your finances and family, for you have no fear of loss.

"Everything depends on whether or not you use your pain correctly. Then there is growth, understanding and never again any such thing as a sense of loss. There is only change, which is the reality of Life, which is happiness.

"Regardless of your relationship with another you must remain psychologically detached from them. This means everyone. You owe nothing to others except to be real, and

147

they owe nothing but the same to you. Do not expect anything else for you alone can only give true value to yourself. This is not cold indifference, rather it is something extraordinarily warm. For it is genuine love. When you learn to do this, everything changes, because you no longer make conscious or unconscious demands upon another."

The man thought of all the demands he had made on others that had been so important to him at the time. Yet, where had they all got him? He had ended up lost and completely alone.

"*Can't you at least help me? It's impossible for me to find that much money. Why didn't you warn me?*" He was sure that the amount was wrong. How could he owe so much tax?

"*I have already done the best I can. And I have been warning you that this would happen. You've just been spending more than you have been earning. It's that simple!*" The accountant's words fell on deaf ears. He had not been listening. It had not been what he had wanted to hear.

"*But it was your idea that I show a big profit,*" he saw himself snap back. "*How can it be on paper, anyway, if I've not seen it?*"

"*You specifically instructed to me to show the best possible figures in order that you could get the mortgage you wanted and I did that from the information you provided.*"

He could not believe what was happening. His house had been repossessed and his creditors had filed for his bankruptcy. He was completely lost and alone. No-one had been even remotely sympathetic. In fact he was certain that they had been pleased about what had happened to him. Even that waiter, who he had always tipped so well, haughtily returned his refused credit card. His embarrassment had hurt terribly as he had tried to blazon it out in front of his colleagues, whilst remarking that he couldn't understand why, and that he would arrange for cash that day.

*

The man now observed himself in a more detached way than he had previously. He was surprised at how helpless and lost he had looked. Had he really been that unaware as to how he had behaved? Surely he could not have been. Yet, watching himself he could see that he was still holding on to his stupid pride.

He thought he had lost everything, his home and family, even his children were becoming strangers; his business, his creditworthiness and his self-respect, but he had not. He had not lost his Pride, which now seemed to find refuge in his self-pity.

"Why did I not see what I was doing to myself?" he asked.

"People's frantic attempts to bring Life to their doorstep," the voice replied, "are the very things that keep it away. In your eyes you were acting in the only way you knew how. You developed a rôle for yourself which was consistent with what you were most familiar. And you continued to act out that rôle even though it was leading you away from all that was available to you."

"But you said that adversity is a way to knock people from their course. Well I had plenty of that didn't I?"

"The quality or quantity of lessons are irrelevant. You must choose to learn. This is not easy when you have delegated your choice to habits that were formed long ago. The habits that you allowed to form throughout your life end up controlling your life. If you don't conquer your habits they always conquer you. For example your habit of only hearing what you wanted to hear simply filtered out the countless warning messages which were sent to you."

The man was quiet as he continued to observe himself with a sadness as to what might have been had he listened more.

•

He poured himself another drink as he looked at his surroundings. Who cared if he was drinking too much, he certainly didn't. All those years of striving to be somebody and where had he arrived? A small cottage. He wondered if his Pride would let him register for assistance. "I'll have to, soon", he thought, the rest of his family had had to, so why not him? Anyway, the rent would need paying.

Funny, he thought, he used to wish to live in a small cottage and now here he was, although this was hardly what he had imagined. Mind you, what had he imagined about anything? His whole life had been one of just getting by from pillar to post. Perhaps he had always been on the look out for what was in it for him, but who didn't? He was certain, though, that he didn't deserve this.

Looking down at the newspaper on the floor he noticed, once more, the 'notice to creditors' insertion about himself in the liquidation's column. That was it. He was bankrupt. What the hell am I going to do? he asked himself. "I might as well kill myself," he said out loud.

"Everyone would be better off without me, probably wouldn't even be missed. It would certainly teach them all. They'd all feel bad about what they had done to me, then, wouldn't they? But he knew he lacked the courage to do it.

As he swallowed his drink, and poured himself another, he noticed an article that he had overlooked before. It was telling the success story of someone he knew. "That's ridiculous!", he shouted. "What the hell has he done to deserve that? It's only because of who he knows, I'll bet!"

*

"Why did I find it so difficult to accept responsibility?" the man asked.

"Your ego was comfortable in the security it had already found for you. This was in believing that it was other people and conditions, beyond its control, which made life the way it was, rather than seeking an alternative security. In blaming others for things not going your way it discovered an acceptable reason for your limited success.

"It allowed your more dominant negative emotions to have control over your thinking," the voice continued. "These emotions took their strength from attaching meaning to external events. Consequently, the way you perceived your world made you externally influenced. When things went well you believed it was good luck. When things went badly, however, you believed the system had it in for you, it was to blame."

"I can see now that I was always looking for reasons, excuses I suppose."

"Immediately you stop making excuses you begin to take complete responsibility for yourself. Responsibility looks forwards, blame always looks backwards."

·

He was determined to see them, if it were the last thing he did, he told himself. They were his children and he had a right to see them. He wanted to explain. He must explain. Make her listen. He drove in the direction where his wife was now living. He was driving fast, but he had to get there as soon as he could. This couldn't wait. Things had to be said, he wanted them all back. If she could just see how sorry he was, he was sure that she would forgive him. She had to, he didn't know where else to turn. The drink may have given him the courage to face them, but, face them he was going to. Everything would be all right. She would listen.

·

"If, because of my choices, I wasted the opportunity to

learn from my life's lessons, how could I grow? Surely my whole life was just a mockery?"

"Whatever situations, your imbalance brings to pass, will continue to arise in different ways until you do grow. How can your life be wasted when it forms only part of your spirit's quest? Opportunity after opportunity will always come. Your spirit will simply wait until the opportunities presented are the ones you do choose to learn from. It knows fulfilment will come. The Law makes it so. It is what God wants for you."

*

He desperately tried to control the car as it skidded towards the crash barrier. Why did it have to be raining so heavily? It all seemed in slow motion as the man observed it now. He had not been going that fast, had he? The bend must have been sharper than he had judged. "Oh my God no!" He heard himself shout, as the oncoming lorry ploughed into his car.

"Why *did* you kill yourself?"

Again the voice asked the question.

She now knew the answer. She would not make the same mistakes as before. Not with *this* opportunity. The Life, the one that the voice had helped her to so vividly recall, had *not* been wasted. She *had* learned. She had *listened*. She *would* choose differently this time.

"In your own time...," the voice calmly intoned, "... open your eyes and breathe deeply."

She became conscious of the soft beating of her heart, the murmur of distant traffic, and the faint silhouette of someone sitting alongside her. The air tasted clean and clinical. Her fingers felt the buttoned recesses of the leather couch.

Steadily, through the darkness, her eyes saw light. The young woman sat up, swung her legs onto the floor and walked towards the rays of sunlight just beginning to stream through the window.

It had been raining heavily and she wanted to touch the rainbow brightening the horizon. Everything was refreshed, washed anew. It glistened and sparkled. She felt *part* of it all. Part of a far *greater* and meaningful quest. A quest that involved her living, learning and growing. And *yes*, she would continue to grow. For now, she understood. The Spirit *within* her would *continue* to seek fulfilment through her. It was what Life was about. It was what she had been made for.

The silhouette's wrist watch continued to silently measure time.

*For every then, there is a now,*

*To delight in beauty, witness grotesque,*

*To reach height, understand depth,*

*To recognise full, first meet empty,*

*For every quest, a why and how,*

*Then believe,*

*with death, comes Life*

*And with Faith, fulfilment.*

**COLIN TURNER**

FINANCIAL FREEDOM
The Principles of Networking: The Right and Wrong Way

This invaluable book explains the principles and practices behind the powerful business concept of networking.

One of the most natural and healthy feelings in the world is enthusiasm. When we are enthusiastic about something, we just *have* to share it with others. It is sharing which is at the heart of successful networking.

Colin Turner shows that, as a vehicle for taking you towards financial independence, even with little or no capital, networking works. *Really works*. Explaining the principles behind this, *Financial Freedom* will help to put you on the right track for success and enable you to fulfil your true business potential.

'*Financial Freedom* is a good, honest guide for networking success' *Evening Standard*

'Networking is probably the most natural and convenient way to do business' B.T.

(Published in January 1999)
HODDER AND STOUGHTON PAPERBACKS

# COLIN TURNER

## SWIMMING WITH PIRANHA
## MAKES YOU HUNGRY
### How to Simplify Your Life and Achieve
### Financial Independence

*Swimming With Piranha Makes You Hungry* is a metaphorical must for anyone desiring to ensure their long-term security.

This unique book provides the powerful and practical advice essential for those seeking to enjoy life more, work less and have more money!

- Learn the laws vital for financial independence
- Discover the secrets to saving money
- Streamline your home, work, lifestyle and health
- Recognise new opportunities every day
- Guaranteed to improve the quality of your life

'Brilliant!' *Daily Mail*

'Highly recommended' *Financial Times*

'Sound advice' *Sunday Independent*

HODDER AND STOUGHTON PAPERBACKS